A Vegan Taste of Eastern Europe

ALSO BY LINDA MAJZLIK

Vegan Baking

Vegan Barbecues and Buffets

Vegan Dinner Parties

A Vegan Taste of The Caribbean

A Vegan Taste of France

A Vegan Taste of Greece

A Vegan Taste of India

A Vegan Taste of Italy

A Vegan Taste of Mexico

A Vegan Taste of The Middle East

A Vegan Taste of North Africa

A Vegan Taste of Thailand

A Vegan Taste of Eastern Europe

Linda Majzlik

Jon Carpenter

Our books may be ordered from bookshops or (post free) from
Jon Carpenter Publishing, Alder House, Market Street, Charlbury,
England OX7 3PH

Credit card orders may be phoned or faxed to 01689 870437
or 01608 811969

First published in 2004 by
Jon Carpenter Publishing
Alder House, Market Street, Charlbury, Oxfordshire OX7 3PH
☎ 01608 811969

ISBN 1 897766 93 9

Printed in England by J. W. Arrowsmith Ltd., Bristol

CONTENTS

INTRODUCTION

The political map of Eastern Europe may have changed considerably in recent times, but one thing that has remained constant is the region's love of home-cooked flavourful dishes made from fresh seasonal produce. Certain foods such as hearty soups topped with dumplings, robust stews and casseroles, dense wholesome rye breads, sweet and savoury stuffed pancakes, fiery horseradish sauce, pickled vegetables, speciality grain dishes, beetroot salads, savoury little pastries and a whole host of desserts, pastries and cakes made with fresh and dried fruits, nuts and poppy seeds, are all immediately identifiable as typically Eastern European. Likewise, the lavish use of the distinctive flavourings of paprika, dill, caraway seeds, sour cream and yoghurt helps to provide the region with its unique culinary identity.

With much of the northern area having a continental climate and the more southerly parts enjoying warmer winters due to the Mediterranean influence, a wide range of crops is produced, many of which are exported. The main cereals grown throughout the region, wheat, rye, barley, millet and maize, are put to good use in a range of traditional recipes. Wheat, rye and maize are milled and made into characteristic breads, without which no meal is considered complete.

Winter-hardy crops such as root vegetables and cabbages form the mainstay of the northern diet, whereas warmer weather produce such as aubergines, courgettes, peppers, tomatoes and olives give the southern region's dishes an altogether more Mediterranean flavour. Many Eastern European recipes are based on traditional peasant-style culinary concoctions and these dishes originated in the days when food needed to be hearty and filling to sustain the farm labourers working the land by hand, long before machinery was introduced. The emphasis in all of the countries is very much on preserving all types of produce, so vegetables are traditionally dried, pickled or bottled for use when they are not available fresh.

The orchards of central and southern parts of Eastern Europe are very productive and a wide variety of fruit is grown, including apples, pears, plums, apricots and cherries, all of which are enjoyed fresh when in season and preserved by bottling or drying. Jams are also made from the bounty of summer fruits, both in the home and on a commercial basis. Almonds, chestnuts, hazelnuts and walnuts are all grown in certain areas and feature in both sweet and savoury recipes. Hungary, Slovakia, Bulgaria and Romania are also noted for their vineyards and they produce good quality wines, some of which are made without animal-derived ingredients in the fining process.

Although a wide range of meat-free dishes is enjoyed on certain days of the year for religious reasons, many people still find it hard to believe that anyone would avoid meat by choice and the concept of veganism is not widely understood. This situation is slowly changing though and in some areas, especially in the cities, there is a growing understanding of the animal-free diet. Meat-free dishes are therefore beginning to appear on the menus of some restaurants, which is good news for travelling vegans. But with all the basic ingredients highly suitable for the vegan diet and dairy-free alternatives to even sour cream increasingly available, there is now also plenty of scope to sample the delights of Eastern European cuisine for vegans who wish to stay at home.

THE VEGAN EASTERN EUROPEAN STORECUPBOARD

As preserving summer fruits by bottling, drying and making them into jam, and drying, bottling and pickling vegetables are all traditional, the typical Eastern European storecupboard is likely to contain a vast array of home-preserved goods alongside the following ingredients.

Almonds Grown in the Balkan region, almonds are widely used in sweet dishes and occasionally in savoury recipes. They are a rich source of protein, vitamins in the B complex, vitamin E and calcium, and their flavour is enhanced if they are lightly toasted.

Apricots Grown in central and southern parts of Europe, the dried fruits are added to savoury dishes or cooked to a thick purée and used as a filling in sweet pastries. Apricots are rich in iron, fibre, vitamins and minerals. Choose plump, unsulphured varieties for the best flavour.

Barley Plainly cooked or mixed with other ingredients, barley is commonly served as an accompaniment or used when making hearty soups. Whole or pot barley is more nutritious than pearl, as it has not been stripped of nutrients in the milling process.

Beans Many varieties are used, with some of the most popular being cannellini, butter, haricot and kidney beans. They are a common ingredient in soups and salads, and are also mixed with grains or mashed and used as spreads, or served plainly cooked as an accompaniment. All beans are a good source of protein, fibre and minerals and it is a good idea to cook them in bulk as they can be frozen successfully.

Breadcrumbs Used as an ingredient and as a topping, breadcrumbs are easily made by whizzing chunks of bread in a food processor or nutmill. Breadcrumbs can be stored in the freezer and used from frozen.

Buckwheat Widely grown in Eastern Europe, buckwheat can be bought ready roasted or unroasted. To roast plain buckwheat, simply put it in a heavy-based pan over a medium heat and stir it around for a couple of minutes. Buckwheat is a seed and not a true grain and the plants belong to the same family as sorrel and rhubarb. The seeds are, however, treated as a grain and served plainly cooked or mixed with other ingredients as an accompaniment, especially in Poland.

Buckwheat flour Milled from whole buckwheat, the flour is greyish in colour and traditionally used to make little savoury pancakes.

Bulgar wheat Although it is widely used in Bulgaria, the name of this crushed wheat actually comes from Turkey. Bulgar can be served plain or mixed with other ingredients as an accompaniment to stews and casseroles.

'Cheese' Used in a variety of recipes as an ingredient or a garnish. Vegan white 'cheese' alternatives made from soya make good substitutes.

Chestnut purée Used throughout the region in sweet dishes, chestnut purée is available tinned, either sweetened or unsweetened.

Chickpea flour A fine, yellowy very nutritious flour made from chickpeas. It is traditionally used in Bulgaria to make delicious savoury buns.

Chickpeas A favourite ingredient all over the Balkans, chickpeas are a good source of protein, fibre, vitamins and minerals. With their creamy, nutty flavour they combine well with all other ingredients and are used in soups, casseroles and salads.

Cooking oils Mildly flavoured vegetable and sunflower oils are favoured in northern areas of Eastern Europe for cooking and making dressings.

Cornflour A very fine starchy white flour milled from maize. It is sometimes known as cornstarch and is used to thicken sauces.

Cornmeal Maize is widely grown in Romania and much of it is used to produce cornmeal from which cornbread and savoury cornmeal balls and also mamaliga, the Romanian version of Italy's polenta, are made.

Country soup mix A nutritious mixture of whole and flaked grains, lentils, beans and peas which is used to make thick soups and filling stews.

'Cream cheese' Used in both sweet and savoury recipes, an excellent vegan alternative made from soya is available from health food stores.

Dried chestnuts Gathering chestnuts in the autumn is a favourite pastime for many Eastern Europeans and these are often dried as a way of preserving them. Dried chestnuts need to be soaked in boiling water for an hour, then simmered for about 45 minutes until tender.

Dried fruit A nutritious mixture of fruits such as apples, apricots, peaches, pears and prunes, which is commonly used to make fruit compotes during the winter months when fresh fruits are scarce.

Dried mushrooms Highly regarded for their rich, intense flavour, dried mushrooms need reconstituting in warm water before use. Although expensive they are only used in small quantities.

Filo pastry Made from flour, salt and water, filo pastry is best bought, either frozen or chilled, as it is difficult and time-consuming to make. It is used here to make a typical savoury strudel and little stuffed pastries. The sheets need to be brushed with oil before cooking.

Gherkins A variety of small cucumber, pickled and sold in jars. They are used to add their distinctive sweet-sour flavour to salads.

Golden syrup Sweet and delicate in taste, this thick syrup is made from molasses residue that has been clarified. It is used in various cake, biscuit and dessert recipes in place of honey.

Hazelnuts These are grown in southern parts of Eastern Europe and are a favourite ingredient all over the region, especially in cakes and desserts. Hazelnuts are best bought whole for grinding or chopping at home and their flavour is enhanced if lightly toasted.

Herbs Some herbs such as dill are only ever used fresh, while others are used both fresh and dried.

Bay leaves The aromatic dried leaves of an evergreen tree are added to soups, casseroles and grain dishes to impart their distinct, strong and slightly bitter taste. The dried leaves are more flavourful than fresh ones.

Chives Used to impart a mild and subtle oniony flavour, chives are often combined with other herbs or snipped and used as a garnish.

Dill The most commonly used herb in Eastern Europe, the feathery leaves of dill with their subtle aniseed flavour are always used fresh.

Marjoram This tiny-leafed herb has a very distinct, aromatic flavour and is often combined with other herbs, especially in Czech cuisine.

Mint Mint has a natural affinity with peas and potatoes and is also used successfully in dishes containing beans, especially in Bulgaria. The whole leaves are used for garnishing and can be added to green salads.

Mixed herbs A mixture of several sweet herbs, usually including rosemary, marjoram and thyme, which is often used dried to flavour dumplings.

Parsley This universally popular herb is used liberally in all kinds of savoury dishes and combines well with other herbs. Fresh parsley is also used for garnishing and the flat-leafed variety is preferred.

Thyme A highly aromatic, small-leafed herb which retains its flavour well when dried. It is especially popular in the Balkan region, where it is combined with mushrooms and tomatoes.

Horseradish The whole fresh roots are not always widely available, but if you are lucky enough to find any they can be peeled and grated, then frozen for longer storage. Jars of grated horseradish, preserved in vinegar, can usually be bought from delicatessen. Horseradish is a member of the same family as mustard and has a very hot and extremely sharp taste. It is commonly mixed with sour cream and used as a condiment, especially in Poland, Slovakia and Hungary.

Jam Eastern Europeans have a great tradition of jam-making and as well as supplying the home market a lot of their jams are exported. Pancakes filled with jam are a very traditional dessert in much of the region and doughnuts filled with jam are a popular snack available from street vendors.

Lemon juice Fresh lemon juice is added to certain soups and savoury dishes and is commonly used in salad dressings.

Lentils Brown and red lentils are used in soups and casseroles and both types combine well with other ingredients. All lentils are a rich source of protein, fibre, vitamins and minerals.

Mayonnaise Some excellent egg-free versions are available from health food stores and some supermarkets. Mayonnaise is an essential ingredient in some salads and is used with pickled cucumbers to make a 'tartare-style' sauce.

Millet Widely grown in parts of Eastern Europe, millet is a highly nutritious, mild-flavoured grain which is served plainly cooked or mixed with other ingredients as an accompaniment.

Molasses A very dark, richly-flavoured, treacly syrup which is a by-product of the sugar-making process. It is rich in iron, vitamins and minerals and is an essential ingredient in dark rye bread.

Olive oil Widely used in the southern parts of Eastern Europe where olives are grown. Olive oil adds its distinctive flavour to various savoury dishes and salad dressings.

Olives are especially popular in Bulgarian and Romanian cuisine.

Pickled cucumber Small firm-textured cucumbers are the type favoured for pickling in dill-flavoured vinegar and these are widely available in jars. They are eaten simply as an accompaniment, or used as a garnish or an ingredient.

Prunes Many kinds of plums are grown in the orchards of Eastern Europe and prunes are the dried fruits of a black-skinned variety. They are a valuable source of iron, calcium and vitamins and are used in both sweet and savoury recipes. Prunes can be bought either pitted or unpitted and the no-need-to-soak type are the most tender.

Rice Long grain rice, either plainly cooked or mixed with other ingredients, makes the perfect accompaniment for stews and casseroles. It is also commonly used as a stuffing for cabbage leaves or as an ingredient in soups. Various creamy desserts are also made with long grain rice.

Rose flower water is popular in Bulgaria, where it is used to flavour desserts. Beware of imitations – authentic flower waters are distilled from real flowers rather than being chemically produced.

Rye flour Rye is grown in northeastern parts of Europe as it is well suited to colder climates. The grain is milled into a greyish coloured, robustly-flavoured flour, which is made into the characteristic dense rye breads of the region. Rye is a good source of vitamin E, B vitamins and minerals.

Sauerkraut Popular throughout Eastern Europe, sauerkraut is finely shredded, pickled, fermented white cabbage, vast quantities of which are made in many homes in special wooden barrels. Sauerkraut is widely available and bottled varieties are preferable to tinned, which often have a slightly metallic taste. As well as being used as an ingredient, sauerkraut is also simply served as a vegetable.

Semolina A nutritious and versatile meal made from durum wheat, semolina is popular in Bulgaria where it is used to make desserts and savoury dumplings.

Silken tofu A soft, smooth-textured variety of tofu which is available in long-life cartons. It blends very easily and is used here to make a substitute for sour cream.

'Sour cream' A vegan alternative made from soya is available, but at the present time does not appear to be stocked in many shops. It may be ordered from some health food stores but if this proves to be difficult a home-made version can easily be made from silken tofu (see page 64).

Soya milk Unsweetened soya milk has been used in both sweet and savoury recipes.

Spices A varied range of spices is used throughout Eastern Europe, some of which make certain dishes immediately identifiable with the region.

Black pepper A universally popular seasoning for savoury dishes. Freshly ground black peppercorns are preferred.

Caraway seed The distinctive aniseed flavour of caraway seed is typical of Eastern European cuisine and it is used in all kinds of savoury dishes and in breads.

Chilli powder The ground dried pods of hot red chillies, chilli powder is used sparingly in some savoury dishes to add 'heat'.

Cinnamon Used in stick form to flavour fruit salads and ground as an ingredient and for sprinkling over sweet dishes.

Cloves The dried buds of an evergreen tree, valued for their anaesthetic and anti-septic qualities. Whole cloves are used to flavour fruit compotes and savoury rice dishes, whilst ground cloves are used sparingly in baked goods.

Dill seed The spice that gives pickled cucumbers their unique flavour, dill seed is also used sparingly to impart its pungent, sweet and aromatic taste to some savoury dishes.

Fennel seed The dried seeds of a plant belonging to the parsley family, fennel imparts an aniseed/licorice flavour and is used in particular in Hungarian potato bread.

Mixed spice A mixture of several sweet spices which is used for flavouring spiced cookies.

Nutmeg The sweet and spicy seed of an evergreen tree, nutmeg is best bought whole and grated as needed. It is used sparingly in vegetable purées and buck-wheat dishes.

Paprika The most widely used spice in Eastern Europe, especially in Hungarian cuisine where it is used to flavour the national dish of goulash. Paprika is the ground dried pod of a sweet red pepper and it adds colour and a mild sweet flavour to savoury dishes, in particular those containing tomatoes.

Poppy seed Black poppy seeds are a favourite ingredient in Hungarian cuisine, where they are ground and used in a filling for sweet pastries. They are also used whole in bread recipes or sprinkled over pastry before baking.

Saffron Made from the dried stigmas of a variety of crocus, saffron is the most expensive of all the spices. Although not common in Eastern European cuisine, it is used sometimes to impart its colour and pungent, slightly bitter, yet aromatic taste to savoury rice dishes.

Textured vegetable protein A nutritious and versatile soya product which readily absorbs the flavours of other ingredients. The natural chunks and minced varieties are used here in various savoury recipes.

Tinned tomatoes Sometimes used in preference to fresh tomatoes when a stronger tomato flavour is desired.

Tomato juice Available in cans or cartons, tomato juice is used in various soups and savoury dishes and any juice left can be frozen.

Tomato purée This strengthens the flavour of and adds colour to tomato-based dishes.

Vegetable stock Used in a variety of savoury recipes, vegetable stock is easy to make and gives a more authentic flavour than stock cubes. It can be made in bulk and frozen in measured quantities. Peel and chop a selection of root vegetables, celery and onion and put them in a pan with a couple of chopped garlic cloves, some black peppercorns, a few sprigs of fresh parsley and a bay leaf. Cover with water and bring to the boil. Simmer covered for 30 minutes. Strain the liquid off through a fine sieve.

Vinegar Red and white wine vinegars are used in dressings for salads and sometimes added to soups and other savoury dishes where an acidic taste is required.

Walnuts Grown in abundance in the Balkan region, walnuts are a favourite ingredient in sweet and savoury recipes. Walnut pieces are cheaper to buy than halves and are ideal for grinding and chopping. Walnuts have been found to have health benefits as they help to lower cholesterol levels in the body.

Wine Bulgaria, Hungary, Slovakia and Romania are all wine producing countries and both red and white wine is occasionally added to savoury recipes. Luckily for vegans, a good selection of wines from these countries are produced without animal ingredients.

Yeast Easy-blend dried yeast is used in pastry and bread recipes here, as it does not need to be reconstituted in liquid.

Yoghurt An essential ingredient in Bulgarian cuisine, where it is claimed that almost everyone eats yoghurt every day. It is used in sweet and savoury recipes and also spooned over foods as a garnish. Plain soya yoghurt makes an excellent substitute.

SOUPS

There is a long tradition in Eastern European countries of making hearty and filling soups and these are perfect for serving with warm crusty bread as light meals. In many households people do not consider a main meal complete without soup as a starter and bowls of soup are often offered as a welcome to guests. Soups are popular even in the summer months and those served then tend to be lighter and often cold and yoghurt-based. Fruit soups are very traditional, especially cherry, and these are very easy to prepare by cooking the chosen fruit to a purée, allowing it to cool and then blending it with yoghurt and water. Some soups are associated with holidays and festivals, such as Polish sweet almond and rice soup, which is traditionally served at Christmas. The origins of borshch are hotly disputed, with opinion divided over which country it originated in. Today it is one of the most popular soups in the region, with all the countries having their own preferred version.

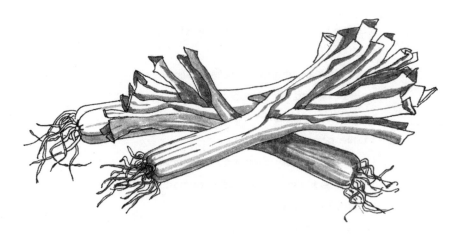

Cauliflower and dill soup (serves 4)

8oz/225g cauliflower, chopped

1 celery stick, trimmed and chopped

1 onion, peeled and chopped

1 garlic clove, crushed

1 dessertspoon vegetable oil

22 fl.oz/650ml vegetable stock

2 rounded tablespoons finely chopped fresh dill

1 dessertspoon lemon juice

1 tablespoon plain soya yoghurt

black pepper

fresh dill leaves

Fry the celery, onion and garlic in the oil in a large pan until softened. Add the cauliflower, stock and chopped dill and season with black pepper. Bring to the boil, cover and simmer for 10-15 minutes until done. Allow to cool slightly, then transfer to a blender and blend smooth. Pour back into the cleaned pan and stir in the lemon juice and yoghurt. Reheat while stirring, then ladle the soup into bowls and garnish with fresh dill leaves.

Celeriac and barley broth (serves 4)

8oz/225g celeriac, peeled and diced

4oz/100g pot barley

4oz/100g leek, trimmed and finely sliced

1 onion, peeled and chopped

1 garlic clove, crushed

1 tablespoon vegetable oil

1 tablespoon finely chopped fresh parsley

1 tablespoon finely chopped fresh marjoram

10 fl.oz/300ml water

16 fl.oz/475ml vegetable stock

black pepper

Put the barley in a pan with the water, cover and leave to soak overnight. Bring to the boil, cover and simmer for 10 minutes. In another large pan, fry the leek, onion and garlic in the oil until soft. Add the barley and remaining cooking liquid, celeriac, parsley, marjoram and stock, season with black pepper and bring to the boil. Cover and simmer, stirring occasionally, for about 25 minutes until the vegetables are cooked and the soup is thick.

Bulgarian bean soup (serves 4)

6oz/175g cooked cannellini beans
4oz/100g tomato, skinned and chopped
4oz/100g carrot, scraped and finely chopped
4oz/100g red pepper, chopped
1 onion, peeled and chopped
1 celery stick, trimmed and finely sliced
1 small red chilli, deseeded and finely chopped
1 dessertspoon vegetable oil
10 fl.oz/300ml vegetable stock
8 fl.oz/225ml tomato juice
2 rounded tablespoons finely chopped fresh mint
1 bay leaf
black pepper
1 dessertspoon lemon juice
fresh mint leaves

Fry the onion, celery and chilli in the oil for 5 minutes in a large pan. Add the tomato and cook until pulpy. Now add the carrot, red pepper, vegetable stock, tomato juice, chopped mint and bay leaf and season with black pepper. Stir well and bring to the boil, cover and simmer for 10 minutes. Add the beans and continue simmering for 10 minutes more, until the vegetables are tender. Stir in the lemon juice and serve garnished with fresh mint leaves.

Brown lentil and vegetable soup (serves 4)

4oz/100g brown lentils

4oz/100g leek, trimmed and sliced

4oz/100g parsnip, peeled and diced

4oz/100g carrot, scraped and diced

1 celery stick, trimmed and sliced

1 onion, peeled and chopped

1 garlic clove, crushed

25 fl.oz/750ml vegetable stock

1 tablespoon vegetable oil

few sprigs of fresh thyme

1 bay leaf

black pepper

chopped fresh parsley

Soak the lentils in boiling water for 2 hours, then drain. Heat the oil in a large pan and fry the leek, parsnip, carrot, celery, onion and garlic for 3 minutes. Add the lentils, stock, bay leaf and thyme and season with black pepper. Stir well and bring to the boil. Cover and simmer for 40-45 minutes, stirring occasionally, until the lentils are done. Ladle the soup into bowls and garnish with chopped fresh parsley.

Polish potato soup (serves 4)

12oz/350g potatoes, peeled and diced

2 celery sticks, trimmed and finely sliced

1 onion, peeled and chopped

1 dessertspoon vegetable oil

2 rounded tablespoons finely chopped fresh parsley

2 bay leaves

black pepper

24 fl.oz/725ml vegetable stock

1 rounded tablespoon vegan 'sour cream'

extra chopped fresh parsley

Fry the celery and onion for 5 minutes in the oil in a large pan. Add the potatoes, parsley, bay leaves and stock and season with black pepper. Stir well and bring to the boil, then cover and simmer for about 15 minutes until cooked. Allow to cool slightly, remove the bay leaves and blend the soup smooth. Rinse the pan, pour the soup back in, stir in the 'sour cream' and gently reheat while stirring. Garnish with chopped parsley when serving.

Apple and pepper soup (serves 4)

8oz/225g eating apples, peeled, cored and chopped

4oz/100g red pepper, chopped

4oz/100g green pepper, chopped

1 celery stick, trimmed and chopped

1 onion, peeled and chopped

1 dessertspoon vegetable oil

20 fl.oz/600ml vegetable stock

1 dessertspoon lemon juice

1 dessertspoon brown sugar

1 bay leaf

black pepper

chopped fresh thyme

Heat the oil in a large pan and fry the peppers, celery and onion for 5 minutes. Add the remaining ingredients except for the thyme and stir well. Bring to the boil, cover and simmer for about 15 minutes until tender. Allow to cool slightly, then blend half of the soup until smooth. Return to the pan and stir well. Reheat and garnish with fresh chopped thyme before serving.

Goulash soup (serves 4)

1lb/450g mixed root vegetables, peeled and finely diced

4oz/100g green pepper, chopped

1 onion, peeled and finely chopped

1 dessertspoon vegetable oil

2 tablespoons finely chopped fresh parsley

1 rounded tablespoon plain soya yoghurt

1 teaspoon paprika

¼ teaspoon caraway seeds

black pepper

5 fl.oz/150ml tomato juice

20 fl.oz/600ml vegetable stock

fresh parsley leaves

Fry the onion in the oil for a couple of minutes, then add the root vegetables, green pepper, chopped parsley, paprika, caraway seeds, tomato juice and vegetable stock. Season with black pepper and stir well, then bring to the boil, cover and simmer for 25 minutes. Allow to cool slightly, blend half of the soup and pour it back into the pan. Stir in the yoghurt and reheat while stirring. Ladle the soup into bowls and garnish with fresh parsley leaves.

Spinach and yoghurt soup (serves 4)

1lb/450g fresh spinach, chopped

1 onion, peeled and chopped

1 tablespoon vegetable oil

15 fl.oz/450ml vegetable stock

1 tablespoon lemon juice

black pepper

4 rounded tablespoons plain soya yoghurt

Soften the onion for 2 minutes in the oil in a large pan, then add the spinach and cook for 3 minutes until wilted. Add the stock and bring to the boil, cover and simmer for 10 minutes. Leave to cool slightly, add the lemon juice and season with black pepper. Transfer to a blender and blend until smooth, then return to the cleaned pan and add the yoghurt. Mix well and gently reheat.

Borshch (serves 4)

8oz/225g raw beetroot, peeled and grated

4oz/100g carrot, scraped and finely chopped

4oz/100g tomato, skinned and chopped

1 celery stick, trimmed and finely sliced

1 onion, peeled and finely chopped

1 garlic clove, crushed

1 dessertspoon vegetable oil

2 rounded tablespoons finely chopped fresh parsley

1 tablespoon red wine vinegar

1 bay leaf

1 teaspoon brown sugar

black pepper

26 fl.oz/775ml vegetable stock

vegan 'sour cream'

fresh dill

Fry the onion, celery and garlic in the oil for 3 minutes. Add the remaining ingredients apart from the 'sour cream' and dill and stir well. Bring to the boil, cover and simmer for about 25 minutes until cooked. Pour about a third of the soup into a blender and blend smooth. Stir into the rest of the soup and gently reheat. Ladle into serving bowls and top with 'sour cream' and fresh dill.

Tomato and rice soup (serves 4)

1lb/450g tomatoes, skinned and chopped

6oz/175g carrot, scraped and grated

4oz/100g long grain rice

1 celery stick, trimmed and finely sliced

1 onion, peeled and chopped

24 fl.oz/725ml water

1 dessertspoon brown sugar

1 dessertspoon tomato purée

1 tablespoon vegetable oil

½ teaspoon paprika

1 bay leaf

black pepper

1 dessertspoon red wine vinegar

chopped fresh parsley

grated vegan 'cheese' (optional)

Put the tomatoes, water and sugar in a pan and bring to the boil. Cover and simmer for 5 minutes, then rub through a sieve into a jug and discard the seeds.

Heat the oil and fry the carrot, celery and onion for 5 minutes. Add the rice, tomato liquid, tomato purée, paprika and bay leaf and season with black pepper. Stir well and bring to the boil, cover and simmer gently for about 15 minutes until the rice is cooked. Stir in the vinegar, ladle the soup into bowls and garnish with grated 'cheese' and chopped parsley.

Cabbage and apple soup (serves 4)

8oz/225g white cabbage, finely shredded

8oz/225g eating apples, peeled, cored and finely chopped

1 onion, peeled and finely sliced

4 rounded tablespoons sauerkraut

1 tablespoon vegetable oil

24 fl.oz/725ml vegetable stock

1 tablespoon lemon juice

1 teaspoon caraway seeds

1 bay leaf

black pepper

chopped walnuts

Fry the cabbage and onion in the oil for 3 minutes, add the remaining ingredients, except the walnuts, and stir well. Bring to the boil, cover and simmer, stirring occasionally, for about 15 minutes until tender. Garnish the bowls of soup with chopped walnuts.

Polish sweet almond and rice soup (serves 4)

4oz/100g ground almonds

3oz/175g long grain rice

1oz/25g raisins, chopped

1 teaspoon almond essence

1 rounded tablespoon brown sugar

24 fl.oz/725ml soya milk

toasted flaked almonds

Cook the rice, drain and put in a large pan with the rest of the ingredients except the flaked almonds. Stir well and bring to the boil while stirring. Continue stirring while simmering for a minute or two until the soup thickens. Garnish with toasted flaked almonds when serving.

Country parsnip soup (serves 4)

8oz/225g parsnip, peeled and diced

4oz/100g country soup mix

1 onion, peeled and chopped

1 celery stick, trimmed and chopped

1 garlic clove, crushed

1 dessertspoon vegetable oil

20 fl.oz/600ml water

5 fl.oz/150ml tomato juice

2 rounded tablespoons finely chopped fresh parsley

1 bay leaf

black pepper

1 dessertspoon white wine vinegar

grated vegan white 'cheese'

Soak the country soup mix in water overnight. Drain and put in a pan with the 20 fl.oz/600ml of water, bring to the boil, cover and simmer for 20 minutes. Strain the cooking liquid into a measuring jug and make up to 15 fl.oz/450ml with water.

Fry the onion, celery and garlic in the oil for 3 minutes. Add the country soup mix, parsnip, measured liquid, tomato juice, parsley and bay leaf. Season with black pepper and stir well. Bring to the boil, cover and simmer, stirring occasionally, for 30 minutes. Remove from the heat and stir in the vinegar. Serve topped with grated 'cheese'.

Courgette, chickpea and spinach soup (serves 4)

8oz/225g courgette, chopped

6oz/175g cooked chickpeas

6oz/175g fresh spinach, chopped

4oz/100g tomato, skinned and chopped

1 onion, peeled and chopped

1 small red chilli, finely chopped

1 rounded tablespoon finely chopped fresh parsley

1 dessertspoon vegetable oil

20 fl.oz/600ml vegetable stock

1 bay leaf

black pepper

1 tablespoon finely chopped fresh dill

1 garlic clove, crushed

1 dessertspoon lemon juice

Heat the oil and soften the onion and chilli. Add the tomato and cook until pulpy, then stir in the stock, courgette, spinach, parsley and bay leaf and season with black pepper. Stir well and bring to the boil, cover and simmer for 10 minutes. Add the chickpeas and continue cooking for another 5 minutes, then remove from the heat and stir in the dill, garlic and lemon juice before ladling into serving bowls.

Cold cucumber, yoghurt and walnut soup
(serves 4)

12oz/350g cucumber, finely chopped or grated

12 fl.oz/350ml plain soya yoghurt

2oz/50g walnuts, finely chopped

1 garlic clove, crushed

8 fl.oz/225ml cold water

2 tablespoons lemon juice

1 rounded tablespoon finely chopped fresh parsley

1 rounded tablespoon finely chopped fresh dill

black pepper

spring onion rings

Mix all the ingredients apart from the spring onion rings until well combined. Ladle the soup into bowls and garnish with spring onion rings.

MAIN COURSES

The countries of Eastern Europe are renowned for their satisfying stews and casseroles, the most famous of which must be goulash, the Hungarian national dish. While all vegetables are suitable for making stews and casseroles, the varieties chosen vary from the hardy root vegetables so popular in the north to the more Mediterranean-inspired flavours in the south, where dishes are likely to include aubergines, courgettes, peppers and tomatoes. The names of some casseroles come from the dish in which they are cooked – Romanian ghiveci is an example of this, called after a large earthenware cooking pot.

Dishes such as stuffed cabbage leaves and savoury pancakes and pastries also feature strongly in all the countries. Banitsa, a spinach-layered pastry, is a traditional favourite in Bulgaria and when this is served on New Year's Eve a cornel twig or small coin is put in, to bring the finder luck throughout the coming year.

Hungarian goulash (serves 4)

1lb/450g tomatoes, skinned and chopped

8oz/225g carrot, scraped and chopped

4oz/100g green pepper, chopped

4oz/100g red pepper, chopped

4oz/100g mushrooms, wiped and sliced

2oz/50g natural textured vegetable protein chunks

1 large onion, peeled and chopped

1 celery stick, trimmed and sliced

2 garlic cloves, crushed

14 fl.oz/425ml hot vegetable stock

1 tablespoon vegetable oil

1 dessertspoon tomato purée

2 dessertspoons paprika

½ teaspoon caraway seeds

black pepper

topping

1½lb/675g potatoes, peeled and thinly sliced

extra vegetable oil

chopped fresh parsley

Soak the vegetable protein chunks in the stock for 30 minutes. Fry the onion, celery and garlic in the oil in a large pan until softened, then add the tomatoes, tomato purée, paprika and caraway seeds and cook gently until pulpy. Stir in the vegetable protein chunks and remaining stock, carrots and green and red peppers, and season with black pepper. Stir well and bring to the boil, then cover and simmer gently for 10 minutes. Meanwhile, boil the potato slices for 3 minutes and drain. Add the mushrooms to the vegetable mixture and spoon into a shallow casserole dish. Arrange the potato slices over the top and brush lightly with vegetable oil. Bake in a preheated oven at 180°C/350°F/Gas mark 4 for 25-30 minutes until browned. Garnish with chopped fresh parsley and serve with vegetables or a salad.

Romanian ghiveci (serves 4)

14oz/400g tin chopped tomatoes

10oz/300g aubergine, diced

8oz/225g potato, peeled and diced

8oz/225g carrot, scraped and chopped

6oz/175g courgette, sliced

6oz/175g cooked red kidney beans

6oz/175g red pepper, sliced

4oz/100g shelled peas

1 onion, peeled and sliced

2 celery sticks, trimmed and sliced

2 garlic cloves, crushed

1 tablespoon olive oil

2 rounded tablespoons chopped fresh mixed herbs (e.g. rosemary, marjoram, thyme)

6 fl.oz/175ml vegetable stock

2 fl.oz/50ml white wine

1 bay leaf

black pepper

chopped fresh parsley

Heat the oil in a large pan and fry the onion, celery and garlic for 2 minutes. Add the potatoes, carrots and stock and bring to the boil, then cover and simmer for 5 minutes. Remove from the heat and add the remaining ingredients except the parsley. Mix thoroughly and transfer to a deep casserole dish. Cover and bake in a preheated oven at 180°C/350°F/Gas mark 4 for about 1½ hours until done. Garnish with fresh parsley and serve with mamaliga and warm bread.

Root vegetable and chickpea casserole with celeriac topping (serves 4)

1lb/450g mixed root vegetables (e.g. carrot, swede, turnip, kohlrabi, potato), peeled and finely diced

8oz/225g leek, trimmed, cut in half lengthways and sliced

8oz/225g cooked chickpeas

1 onion, peeled and sliced

2 garlic cloves, crushed

12 fl.oz/350ml tomato juice

1 tablespoon lemon juice

1 tablespoon vegetable oil

1 tablespoon fresh thyme

1 bay leaf

black pepper

topping

2lb/900g celeriac

squeeze of lemon juice

4 rounded tablespoons plain soya yoghurt

finely chopped fresh parsley

Fry the leek, onion and garlic in the oil for 5 minutes in a large pan. Add the mixed vegetables, tomato juice, lemon juice, thyme and bay leaf and season with black pepper. Stir well and bring to the boil. Cover and simmer, stirring occasionally, for about 15 minutes until the vegetables are almost tender. Remove from the heat and stir in the chickpeas.

Peel and chop the celeriac and boil it in a large pan of water to which a squeeze of lemon juice has been added. Drain and dry off over a low heat, then mash, add the yoghurt and mix thoroughly. Spoon the vegetable and chickpea mixture into a shallow casserole dish and fork the mashed celeriac evenly over the top. Cover and bake in a preheated oven at 180°C/350°F/Gas mark 4 for 30 minutes. Garnish with chopped fresh parsley and serve with a green vegetable accompaniment.

Country vegetable stew with prunes (serves 4)

12oz/350g leek, trimmed and sliced

6oz/175g country soup mix

6oz/175g swede, peeled and diced

6oz/175g carrot, scraped and diced

6oz/175g turnip, peeled and diced

6oz/175g potato, peeled and diced

3oz/75g pitted prunes, chopped

30 fl.oz/900ml water

18 fl.oz/525ml vegetable stock

1 onion, peeled and chopped

2 celery sticks, trimmed and sliced

2 garlic cloves, crushed

1 tablespoon vegetable oil

2 rounded tablespoons finely chopped fresh parsley

½ teaspoon dill seed

black pepper

chopped walnuts

Soak the country soup mix in water overnight. Drain and bring to the boil with the 30 fl.oz/900ml water, then cover and simmer for 20 minutes. Fry the leek, onion, celery and garlic in the oil in a large pan for 3 minutes. Add the country soup mix and remaining cooking liquid, together with the diced vegetables, prunes, vegetable stock, parsley and dill seed. Season with black pepper and stir well. Bring to the boil, cover and simmer, stirring occasionally, for about 30 minutes until the mixture is thick and the vegetables are done. Garnish with chopped walnuts and serve with a green vegetable and warm crusty bread.

Layered red cabbage casserole (serves 4)

1lb/450g red cabbage

12oz/350g carrots, scraped and grated

8oz/225g tomatoes, skinned and chopped

6oz/175g red pepper, chopped

2oz/50g natural minced textured vegetable protein

2 celery sticks, trimmed and finely chopped

1 onion, peeled and chopped

2 garlic cloves, crushed

8 fl.oz/225ml vegetable stock

4 fl.oz/125ml tomato juice

1 dessertspoon vegetable oil

1 dessertspoon tomato purée

½ teaspoon paprika

½ teaspoon dill seed

black pepper

topping

2oz/50g breadcrumbs

1oz/25g walnuts, chopped

Soak the vegetable protein in the stock for 15 minutes. Heat the oil in a large pan and fry the celery, onion and garlic until softened. Add the tomatoes and cook until pulpy, then put in the vegetable protein and remaining stock, carrots, red pepper, tomato juice and purée, paprika and dill seed. Season with black pepper and mix well. Bring to the boil, cover and simmer for 5 minutes, then set aside.

Separate the cabbage leaves and remove all thick stalks. Place the leaves in a large pan of water and bring to the boil. Simmer for 5 minutes, then drain and spread half the leaves in the base of a greased casserole dish of about 12 x 9 inches/30x23cm. Top with half of the vegetable mixture, then repeat these layers. Mix the breadcrumbs with the walnuts and sprinkle evenly over the top, cover with foil and bake in a preheated oven at 180°C/350°F/Gas mark 4 for

20 minutes. Remove the foil and bake for 10 minutes more until golden. Serve with a green vegetable or a salad.

Aubergine, pepper and mushroom stew (serves 4)

1½lb/675g aubergine, diced

8oz/225g mushrooms, wiped and sliced

4oz/100g green pepper, chopped

4oz/100g red pepper, chopped

1 onion, peeled and chopped

2 garlic cloves, crushed

4 tablespoons vegetable oil

½oz/15g dried mushrooms

6 fl.oz/175ml boiling water

4 rounded tablespoons finely chopped fresh parsley

black pepper

2 rounded tablespoons vegan 'sour cream'

extra chopped fresh parsley

Soak the dried mushrooms in the boiling water for 30 minutes. Fry the aubergine, onion and garlic in the oil for 10 minutes, stirring frequently to prevent sticking. Add the dried mushrooms and soaking liquid, fresh mushrooms, green and red pepper and parsley and season with black pepper. Stir well and raise the heat. Cook for about 15 minutes, stirring occasionally, until tender. Add the 'sour cream' and cook for a further minute or two, stirring until heated through. Garnish with chopped parsley and serve with a grain dish and warm bread.

Bulgarian musaka (serves 4)

1lb/450g mixed peppers, chopped

4oz/100g shelled peas

2oz/50g natural minced textured vegetable protein

1 onion, peeled and chopped

1 small red chilli, finely chopped

1 tablespoon olive oil

10 fl.oz/300ml vegetable stock

12 fl.oz/350ml tomato juice

1 teaspoon paprika

1 rounded tablespoon finely chopped fresh parsley

1 rounded tablespoon finely chopped fresh basil

1 bay leaf

black pepper

topping

1½lb/675g potatoes, peeled and finely diced

4 rounded tablespoons plain soya yoghurt

1oz/25g breadcrumbs

Soak the vegetable protein in the stock for 20 minutes. Fry the peppers, onion and chilli in the oil for 5 minutes, then add the vegetable protein and soaking liquid, peas, tomato juice, paprika, parsley, basil and bay leaf and season with black pepper. Stir well, bring to the boil and simmer, stirring occasionally, for 5 minutes. Spoon into a shallow baking dish.

Boil or steam the potatoes, then drain and arrange evenly over the top of the vegetable mixture. Spoon the yoghurt over the potatoes and sprinkle the breadcrumbs on top. Cover with foil and bake in a preheated oven at 180°C/350°F/Gas mark 4 for 25 minutes. Uncover and bake for 5 minutes more until golden brown. Serve with a salad and warm bread.

Aubergine and lentil pie with potato crusts (serves 4)

1lb/450g aubergine, finely diced

8oz/225g tomatoes, skinned and chopped

4oz/100g brown lentils

1 onion, peeled and finely chopped

1 celery stick, trimmed and finely sliced

1 garlic clove, crushed

3 tablespoons vegetable oil

1 tablespoon tomato purée

1 teaspoon paprika

1 teaspoon caraway seed

black pepper

topping

1½lb/675g potatoes, peeled

4oz/100g self raising flour

1 rounded tablespoon vegan margarine

1 dessertspoon dried parsley

Soak the lentils in water overnight, drain and rinse and place in a fresh pan of water. Bring to the boil, cover and simmer for 15 minutes. Drain over a bowl and keep the liquid. Fry the aubergine, onion, celery and garlic in the oil in a large pan, stirring frequently, for 10 minutes. Add the lentils, tomatoes, tomato purée, paprika and caraway seeds and 8 fl.oz/225ml of the cooking liquid. Season with black pepper and stir well. Bring to the boil, cover and simmer, stirring occasionally, for 15 minutes. Transfer the mixture to a shallow casserole dish.

Boil or steam the potatoes, drain and mash with the margarine. Add the flour and parsley and mix thoroughly, then take rounded dessertspoonfuls and roll into balls. Flatten these into rounds and arrange them neatly on top of the vegetable and lentil mixture to cover completely. Bake in a preheated oven at 180°C/350°F/Gas mark 4 for 30-35 minutes until browned. Serve with a green vegetable or a salad.

Baked pancake pudding (serves 4)

pancakes

3½oz/90g plain flour

½oz/15g soya flour

10 fl.oz/300ml soya milk

1 tablespoon vegetable oil

vegan margarine

filling

12oz/350g leeks, trimmed, halved lengthways and finely sliced

8oz/225g frozen cooked chopped spinach, thawed

1 onion, peeled and finely chopped

2 garlic cloves, crushed

4oz/100g vegan 'cream cheese'

2 tablespoons vegetable oil

1 tablespoon finely chopped fresh marjoram

black pepper

vegan 'sour cream'

Whisk the flours with the soya milk and vegetable oil until smooth. Heat a small amount of margarine in an 8 inch/20cm non-stick frying pan until hot and, using about 4½ tablespoonfuls of batter for each one, make 4 pancakes, cooking each side until golden.

Fry the leeks, onion and garlic in the oil for 10 minutes. Add the spinach and cook for another 2 minutes, stirring frequently. Remove from the heat and add the marjoram and 'cream cheese', season with black pepper and mix thoroughly. Put one of the pancakes in a greased loose-bottomed 8 inch/20cm diameter flan tin and spread a third of the filling evenly on top. Repeat these layers twice and top with the remaining pancake. Cover with foil and bake in a preheated oven at 180°C/350°F/Gas mark 4 for 20 minutes, then take off the foil and bake for 10 minutes more. Carefully remove from the tin and cut into 4 wedges. Garnish each wedge with 'sour cream' and serve with vegetable and salad accompaniments.

Stuffed cabbage leaves (serves 4)

16 large green cabbage leaves

filling

4oz/100g long grain rice

2oz/50g natural minced textured vegetable protein

2oz/50g mushrooms, wiped and chopped

1oz/25g raisins

1 onion, peeled and finely chopped

2 celery sticks, trimmed and finely chopped

2 garlic cloves, crushed

1 tablespoon vegetable oil

16 fl.oz/475ml vegetable stock

12 fl.oz/350ml tomato juice

½ teaspoon paprika

½ teaspoon dill seed

black pepper

Soak the vegetable protein for 20 minutes in half the vegetable stock. Fry the onion, celery and garlic in the oil for 5 minutes, then stir in the soaked vegetable protein, rice, mushrooms, raisins, paprika, dill seed and remaining stock. Season with black pepper and stir well, bring to the boil and simmer gently until the liquid has been absorbed. Blanch the cabbage leaves in boiling water for 3 minutes, drain and remove the thick stalks. Divide the filling equally between the leaves, putting it at the top of each leaf. Fold the edges over to enclose the filling and roll the leaves up. Place the rolls in a single layer in a shallow greased casserole dish and pour the tomato juice over them. Cover with foil and bake in a preheated oven at 180°C/350°F/Gas mark 4 for 40 minutes. Serve with a vegetable.

Chestnut and celeriac pie (serves 4/6)

pastry

8oz/225g plain wholemeal flour

pinch of salt

1 teaspoon easy-blend yeast

1 tablespoon sunflower oil

approx. 5 fl.oz/150ml warm water

soya milk

poppy seeds

filling

12oz/350g celeriac, peeled

6oz/175g dried chestnuts

1 onion, peeled and finely chopped

1 garlic clove, crushed

1 tablespoon sunflower oil

2 tablespoons finely chopped fresh parsley

1 rounded tablespoon vegan 'sour cream'

1 teaspoon paprika

black pepper

garnish

vegan 'sour cream'

Soak the chestnuts in boiling water for an hour, drain and rinse and put in fresh water. Bring to the boil, cover and simmer for about 45 minutes until tender. Rinse the chestnuts in cold water and grate them. Cut the celeriac into even-sized chunks and steam until done, then mash it. Fry the onion and garlic in the oil until soft, remove from the heat and add the chestnuts, celeriac, parsley, 'sour cream' and paprika. Season with black pepper and combine very well.

Mix the flour with the salt and yeast in a large bowl, stir in the sunflower oil and gradually add the warm water until a soft dough forms. Knead the dough well and return it to the bowl. Cover and leave to rise in a warm place for 1 hour. Knead the dough on a floured board, then roll out three-quarters of it to line a greased loose-bottomed 8 inch/20cm deep round flan tin. Spoon the filling evenly into the pastry case and roll out the remaining pastry to make a lid. Press the edges of the pastry together with a fork and score the top with a sharp knife into diamond shapes. Make a slit in the centre of each diamond, then leave for 30 minutes to rise. Brush the top with soya milk, sprinkle with poppy seeds and bake in a preheated oven at 170°C/325°F/Gas mark 3 for 30-35 minutes until browned. Cut into wedges and garnish with 'sour cream'. Serve with vegetable accompaniments.

Leek and spinach banitsa (serves 6)

pastry
8oz/225g plain flour

1 tablespoon sunflower oil

1 dessertspoon white wine vinegar

pinch of salt

approx. 5 fl.oz/150ml warm water

extra sunflower oil

filling
1½lb/675g leeks, trimmed, cut in half lengthways and sliced

1lb/450g frozen cooked chopped spinach, thawed

2 celery sticks, trimmed and finely chopped

2 garlic cloves, crushed

2 tablespoons sunflower oil

2oz/50g vegan white 'cheese', grated

4 rounded tablespoons plain soya yoghurt

black pepper

Sift the flour and salt into a mixing bowl, stir in the oil and vinegar and gradually add enough water to form a soft dough. Turn out onto a floured board and knead for 5 minutes until smooth. Return to the bowl, cover and leave for an hour.

Meanwhile make the filling by frying the leeks, celery and garlic in the oil for 15 minutes, stirring frequently. Remove from the heat and add the grated 'cheese'. Put the spinach in a fine sieve and press out any excess liquid, then add it to the leeks together with the yoghurt. Season with black pepper and mix thoroughly. Set aside to cool.

Divide the dough into 4 equal pieces and roll and stretch each piece into an oblong of 12 x 8 inches/30x20cm. Put one sheet of pastry on a greased baking sheet and top with a third of the filling, spreading it out evenly. Repeat these layers twice and finish with the remaining sheet of pastry. Neaten the edges of the pastry to enclose the filling and brush the top with oil. Bake in a preheated oven at 180°C/350°F/Gas mark 4 for about 30 minutes until golden brown. Serve hot with vegetables and salad.

Broccoli- and spinach-stuffed pancakes (serves 4)

pancakes
3½oz/90g plain flour

½oz/15g soya flour

10 fl.oz/300ml soya milk

1 tablespoon vegetable oil

vegan margarine

filling
10oz/300g broccoli, chopped

10oz/300g frozen cooked chopped spinach, thawed

1 onion, peeled and finely chopped

1 dessertspoon vegetable oil

2oz/50g vegan white 'cheese', grated

5 fl.oz/150ml vegetable stock

1 tablespoon finely chopped fresh marjoram

5 fl.oz/150ml soya milk

1 rounded dessertspoon cornflour

black pepper

garnish

vegan 'sour cream'

First make the pancakes. Whisk the two flours with the soya milk and vegetable oil until smooth. Heat a small amount of margarine in an 8 inch/20cm non-stick frying pan and use about 2 tablespoonfuls of batter each to make 8 pancakes. Keep them warm while making the filling.

Fry the onion in the oil until softened, add the broccoli, stock and marjoram and season with black pepper. Bring to the boil and simmer for 5 minutes, then put in the spinach and continue cooking for another few minutes, stirring frequently, until tender. Mix the cornflour with the soya milk and add to the pan together with the 'cheese'. Mix well, then bring to the boil while stirring and continue stirring for a minute or two until the mixture thickens. Divide the filling between the pancakes and roll or fold each one over to enclose it. Spoon some 'sour cream' on top and serve with a vegetable.

Vegetable strudel (serves 6)

10oz/300g packet filo pastry, thawed

vegetable oil

poppy seeds

filling

8oz/225g carrot, scraped and grated

8oz/225g turnip, peeled and grated

8oz/225g tomatoes, skinned and chopped

4oz/100g green pepper, finely chopped

4oz/100g red pepper, finely chopped

1 onion, peeled and finely chopped

1 celery stick, trimmed and finely sliced

2 garlic cloves, crushed

1 dessertspoon vegetable oil

2oz/50g natural minced textured vegetable protein

12 fl.oz/350ml vegetable stock

1 tablespoon tomato purée

1 teaspoon paprika

1 teaspoon caraway seeds

black pepper

Soak the vegetable protein in the stock for 20 minutes. Fry the onion, celery and garlic in the oil until softened. Add the vegetable protein and any remaining soaking liquid together with the remaining filling ingredients, mix well and simmer, stirring frequently, for 10 minutes. Remove from the heat and allow to cool.

Cut the filo sheets in half, then put 3 sheets on top of each other on an oiled baking sheet, lightly brushing between them with vegetable oil. Spread a third of the filling evenly on the pastry, leaving a gap around the edges. Repeat these layers twice and finish with the remaining sheets of filo, again brushing between them with oil. Tuck the pastry edges under to enclose the filling. Brush the top with oil, sprinkle with poppy seeds and bake in a preheated oven at 180°C/350°F/Gas mark 4 for about 25 minutes until golden. Serve with vegetable and salad accompaniments.

Vegetable and lentil casserole with herby dumplings (serves 4)

14oz/400g tin chopped tomatoes

8oz/225g carrot, scraped and diced

8oz/225g potato, peeled and diced

8oz/225g courgette, chopped

4oz/100g red pepper, sliced

4oz/100g green beans, topped, tailed and cut into 1 inch/2.5cm lengths

4oz/100g red lentils

1 onion, peeled and sliced

1 celery stick, trimmed and sliced

16 fl.oz/475ml vegetable stock

1 tablespoon vegetable oil

2 tablespoons finely chopped fresh parsley

1 tablespoon finely chopped fresh marjoram

1 dessertspoon tomato purée

1 bay leaf

¼ teaspoon chilli powder

black pepper

extra chopped fresh parsley

dumplings

4oz/100g self raising flour

1oz/25g vegan margarine

1 rounded teaspoon dried mixed herbs

black pepper

approx. 3 tablespoons soya milk

Rub the margarine into the flour, then stir in the herbs and season with black pepper and add enough soya milk to bind. Knead well, break the dough into 20 equal pieces and roll each one into a small ball.

Heat the oil in a large pan and fry the onion and celery until soft. Add the carrot, potato, lentils and stock and bring to the boil, cover and simmer for 10 minutes. Put in the remaining ingredients apart from the extra parsley and stir well. Bring back to the boil, then transfer to a deep round casserole dish. Arrange the dumplings on top and press them in lightly until they are just below the surface. Cover and bake in a preheated oven at 180°C/350°F/Gas mark 4 for 1 hour. Garnish with fresh parsley and serve with a green vegetable or a salad.

ACCOMPANIMENTS

Potatoes in their many guises are one of the most popular accompaniments to main courses throughout the region and these are served baked, boiled, fried or mashed with sour cream or yoghurt and flavoured with chopped fresh herbs. They are also made into dumplings, especially in the Czech Republic and Slovakia, and these are perfect for serving with soups, stews and casseroles. Cabbage also is never off the menu in central and northern areas and this is usually boiled, fried, sautéed or baked in the oven. Gathering mushrooms is popular with many Eastern Europeans and these are very often fried with garlic and then mixed with sour cream and fresh dill.

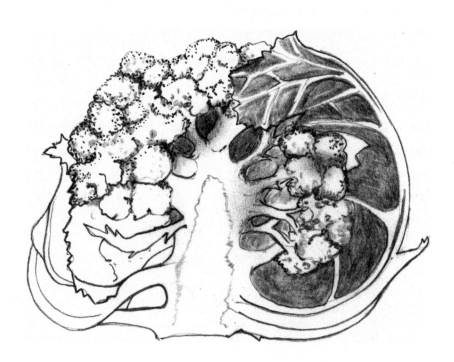

Boiled potato and semolina dumplings (serves 4)

1¼lb/550g potatoes, peeled and cut into chunks

4oz/100g semolina

black pepper

24 fl.oz/725ml vegetable stock

Boil the potatoes, drain and dry off over a low heat. Mash them and season with black pepper, then add the semolina. Mix thoroughly and shape rounded dessertspoonfuls of the mixture into balls, put these on a plate, cover and chill for a couple of hours. Bring the stock to the boil in a saucepan. Add the dumplings and simmer for 10 minutes. Remove them with a slotted spoon and serve with soups, casseroles or stews.

Steamed potato dumplings (serves 4)

1¼lb/550g potatoes, peeled

2oz/50g plain flour

1 rounded teaspoon dried mixed herbs

black pepper

Cut the potatoes into even-sized chunks and boil for 10 minutes. Drain and allow to cool, then grate them into a mixing bowl. Add the flour and herbs, season with black pepper and mix until everything binds together. Take rounded dessertspoonfuls of the mixture and shape into balls. Steam the dumplings for 5 minutes, then serve as an accompaniment to soups, stews or casseroles.

Carrot and swede purée (serves 4)

12oz/350g carrot, scraped and diced

12oz/350g swede, peeled and diced

1 rounded dessertspoon vegan margarine

½ teaspoon paprika

black pepper

Boil the carrot and swede until done, then drain and dry off over a low heat. Mash the vegetables with the margarine and add the paprika, season with black pepper and mix thoroughly. Spoon into an ovenproof dish and fork over the top. Cover and put in a preheated oven at 180°C/350°F/Gas mark 4 for 10-15 minutes until heated through.

Potato and apple purée (serves 4)

1lb/450g potatoes, peeled

8oz/225g eating apples, peeled, cored and chopped

1 tablespoon water

1 teaspoon lemon juice

1 rounded tablespoon vegan margarine

pinch of grated nutmeg

black pepper

1 small red-skinned eating apple, cored and sliced

extra lemon juice

Boil the potatoes, drain, dry off over a low heat and mash with the margarine. Put the chopped apple, teaspoonful of lemon juice and water into a small pan and cook until soft. Mash the apple smooth and add to the potato, together with the nutmeg. Season with black pepper and mix well. Spoon the purée into an ovenproof dish and fork over the top, then cover and place in a preheated oven at 180°C/350°F/Gas mark 4 for 10-15 minutes until heated through. Sprinkle the apple slices with lemon juce and use to garnish the purée before serving.

Celeriac and potato purée (serves 4)

1lb/450g celeriac, peeled

1lb/450g potatoes, peeled

lemon juice

1 tablespoon vegan margarine

2 tablespoons soya milk

black pepper

Cut the celeriac and potatoes into even-sized chunks and cook them in a pan of water to which some lemon juice has been added. Drain and dry off over a low heat. Mash with the margarine, stir in the soya milk and season with black pepper. Spoon the purée into an ovenproof dish and fork over the top. Cover and heat through in a preheated oven at 180°C/350°F/Gas mark 4 for 10-15 minutes.

Green beans with yoghurt and dill (serves 4)

1lb/450g green beans, topped, tailed and cut into 1 inch/2.5cm lengths

1 onion, peeled and finely chopped

1 dessertspoon vegetable oil

4 fl.oz/125ml vegetable stock

2 tablespoons finely chopped fresh dill

1 tablespoon white wine vinegar

black pepper

2 rounded tablespoons plain soya yoghurt

extra fresh dill

Fry the onion in the oil for a few minutes, then add the beans, stock, chopped dill and vinegar. Season with black pepper and bring to the boil. Cover and simmer for about 10 minutes until tender. Add the yoghurt and stir around for a minute or so, then transfer to a serving dish and garnish with fresh dill.

Peas with tomatoes (serves 4)

10oz/300g shelled peas

8oz/225g tomatoes, peeled and finely chopped

1 onion, peeled and finely chopped

1 dessertspoon vegetable oil

1 tablespoon finely chopped fresh marjoram

1 tablespoon water

½ teaspoon paprika

black pepper

finely chopped fresh parsley

Heat the oil and fry the onion until soft. Add the tomatoes and stir around for 1 minute, then put in the peas, marjoram, water and paprika. Season with black pepper and cook, stirring occasionally, for 10 minutes. Spoon into a serving dish and garnish with fresh parsley.

Hungarian-style spinach (serves 4)

1¼lb/550g fresh spinach

1 onion, peeled and finely chopped

1 garlic clove, crushed

1 tablespoon vegetable oil

7 fl.oz/200ml soya milk

1 rounded dessertspoon cornflour

black pepper

Wash and chop the spinach and cook gently in a large pan with only the water that clings to the leaves. Drain and press out any excess water. Fry the onion and garlic in the oil until soft. Combine the cornflour with the soya milk and add to the pan together with the spinach, season with black pepper and stir well. Bring to the boil while stirring and continue stirring for a minute or two until the mixture thickens.

Romanian leeks with olives (serves 4)

1¼lb/550g leeks, trimmed

2 garlic cloves, crushed

8 black olives, sliced

1 tablespoon finely chopped fresh thyme

1 tablespoon olive oil

1 dessertspoon tomato purée

3 fl.oz/75ml white wine

black pepper

chopped fresh parsley

Cut the leeks in half lengthways and then into 1 inch/2.5cm slices. Fry these with the garlic in the oil for 5 minutes. Dissolve the tomato purée in the wine and add, together with the thyme. Season with black pepper and cook, stirring occasionally, for 8 minutes. Add the olives and continue cooking for 2-3 minutes until the leeks are done. Serve garnished with fresh parsley.

Braised carrot with celery (serves 4)

10oz/300g carrots, scraped

6oz/175g celery, trimmed

4 fl.oz/125ml vegetable stock

1 tablespoon vegetable oil

2 rounded tablespoons finely chopped fresh parsley

black pepper

celery leaves

Cut the carrots and celery into 1 inch/2.5cm matchsticks and fry them in the oil for 5 minutes. Add the stock and parsley and season with black pepper. Stir well and bring to the boil, then simmer for 10-12 minutes until tender. Transfer to a serving bowl and garnish with celery leaves.

Paprika potatoes (serves 4)

1½lb/675g potatoes, peeled and diced

6oz/175g tomatoes, skinned and chopped

4oz/100g green pepper, chopped

1 small onion, peeled and finely chopped

1 garlic clove, crushed

1 dessertspoon vegetable oil

1 dessertspoon tomato purée

1 teaspoon paprika

¼ teaspoon caraway seeds

black pepper

2 tablespoons water

finely chopped fresh parsley

Heat the oil and fry the green pepper, onion and garlic until soft. Put in the tomatoes, tomato purée, paprika, caraway seeds and water and season with black pepper, stir well and cook gently for 3 minutes. Boil the potatoes until just done, then drain and add. Spoon into a baking dish, cover with foil and bake in a preheated oven at 180°C/350°F/Gas mark 4 for 20 minutes. Garnish with chopped parsley when serving.

Cauliflower polonaise (serves 4)

1lb/450g cauliflower, cut into florets

1oz/25g breadcrumbs

½oz/15g vegan margarine

chopped fresh parsley

Steam the cauliflower until tender. Meanwhile melt the margarine in a small pan, add the breadcrumbs and stir around until golden. Spoon the cauliflower into a warmed serving dish, scatter the breadcrumbs on top and garnish with fresh parsley.

Baked root vegetables (serves 4)

1½ lb/675g mixed root vegetables (e.g. swede, carrot, parsnip, potato, kohlrabi, turnip), peeled and diced

1 onion, peeled and finely chopped

1 dessertspoon vegetable oil

6 fl.oz/175ml soya milk

2 tablespoons finely chopped fresh parsley

1 rounded teaspoon cornflour

black pepper

chopped walnuts

Boil the vegetables for 10 minutes, then drain. Fry the onion in the oil until softened. Combine the cornflour with the soya milk and add to the onion together with the parsley, season with black pepper and bring to the boil while stirring. Continue stirring for 1 minute, then remove from the heat and add the vegetables. Mix well and transfer to a casserole dish. Cover tightly with foil and bake in a preheated oven at 180°C/350°F/Gas mark 4 for 40 minutes. Garnish with chopped walnuts.

Bulgarian layered aubergine and tomato (serves 4)

12oz/350g aubergine, cut into ¼ inch/5mm slices

14oz/400g tin chopped tomatoes

1 onion, peeled and chopped

4oz/100g red pepper, chopped

1 garlic clove, crushed

2 tablespoons finely chopped fresh parsley

½ teaspoon paprika

black pepper

1 dessertspoon olive oil

extra olive oil

extra chopped fresh parsley

Heat the dessertspoonful of oil and fry the onion, red pepper and garlic until soft. Take off the heat and add the tomatoes, 2 tablespoonfuls of parsley and paprika, season with black pepper and stir well.

Brush the aubergine slices on both sides with olive oil and put them on a baking sheet under a hot grill for a few minutes until softened, turning once. Spoon a third of the tomato mixture into a baking dish and top with half the aubergine slices. Repeat these layers and finish with a tomato layer. Cover and bake in a preheated oven at 180°C/350°F/Gas mark 4 for 25 minutes. Serve warm or cold, sprinkled with chopped parsley.

Courgette and tomato bake (serves 4)

12oz/350g courgettes, sliced

12oz/350g tomatoes, sliced

2 garlic cloves, crushed

2 dessertspoons olive oil

2 rounded tablespoons finely chopped fresh parsley

black pepper

1oz/25g breadcrumbs

½oz/15g walnuts, finely chopped

1 rounded teaspoon vegan margarine

extra chopped fresh parsley

Fry the courgettes and garlic in the olive oil for 2 minutes, then arrange them in a shallow ovenproof dish. Sprinkle with parsley and season with black pepper and layer the tomatoes on top. Sprinkle these with more parsley and season with black pepper. Melt the margarine in a small pan and stir in the breadcrumbs and walnuts. Sprinkle this mixture evenly over the tomatoes and cover the dish with foil. Bake in a preheated oven at 180°C/350°F/Gas mark 4 for 30 minutes. Remove the foil and return to the oven for 5 minutes more until golden brown. Garnish with chopped parsley when serving.

Red cabbage with apple (serves 4)

12oz/350g red cabbage, finely shredded

1 eating apple, peeled, cored and diced

1 onion, peeled and sliced

1 garlic clove, crushed

1 tablespoon vegetable oil

2 tablespoons red wine

2 tablespoons red wine vinegar

3 fl.oz/75ml water

1 teaspoon caraway seeds

black pepper

Fry the cabbage, onion and garlic for 3 minutes in the oil in a large pan. Add the wine, wine vinegar, water and caraway seeds and season with black pepper. Bring to the boil, cover and simmer for 10 minutes, then put in the apple and stir well. Continue simmering, stirring occasionally, for another 10 minutes until cooked.

Hungarian peppers with tomatoes (serves 4)

1lb/450g mixed peppers, thinly sliced

14oz/400g tin chopped tomatoes

1 onion, peeled and sliced

1 tablespoon vegetable oil

1 teaspoon paprika

1 teaspoon brown sugar

black pepper

chopped fresh parsley

Fry the peppers and onion in the oil for 5 minutes. Add the tomatoes, paprika and sugar and season with black pepper. Bring to the boil, cover and simmer for about 25 minutes, stirring occasionally, until tender. Garnish with chopped parsley.

SAUCES

Many of the typical Eastern European sauces are made from basic storecupboard ingredients and do not involve any complicated cooking techniques. Savoury sauces are ideal for spooning over plain boiled vegetables, especially potatoes and other root vegetables, and they instantly add an authentic flavour. 'Sour cream' is a staple in many of the countries and is used both as an ingredient in various recipes and as a topping for savoury and sweet dishes. Likewise, horseradish sauce is widely used as a condiment with either hot or cold foods. Sweet dessert sauces are extremely popular, especially in central areas where they are commonly served with pancakes, sweet dumplings and pastries.

Onion and paprika sauce (serves 4)

4oz/100g onion, peeled and finely chopped

1 dessertspoon vegetable oil

1 rounded teaspoon paprika

black pepper

8 fl.oz/225ml vegetable stock

2 fl.oz/50ml soya milk

1 rounded dessertspoon cornflour

Fry the onion in the oil for 10 minutes, then add the stock and paprika and season with black pepper. Bring to the boil, cover and simmer for 5 minutes. Mix the cornflour with the soya milk until smooth, add to the pan and stir well. Bring to the boil while stirring and continue stirring for a minute or so until the sauce thickens.

Lemon and dill sauce (serves 4)

10 fl.oz/300ml soya milk

½oz/15g vegan margarine

½oz/15g cornflour

2 tablespoons lemon juice

2 tablespoons finely chopped fresh dill

black pepper

Melt the margarine in a small pan, add the cornflour and mix until smooth. Remove from the heat and stir in the soya milk, lemon juice and dill. Season with black pepper and whisk until no lumps remain. Return to the heat, bring to the boil while stirring and continue stirring for a minute or so until the sauce thickens.

Tomato and wine sauce (serves 4)

14oz/400g tin crushed tomatoes

1 onion, peeled and finely chopped

1 stick of celery, trimmed and finely chopped

1 garlic clove, crushed

4 fl.oz/125ml red wine

1 dessertspoon olive oil

2 rounded tablespoons finely chopped fresh parsley

black pepper

Heat the oil and fry the onion, celery and garlic for 5 minutes. Add the remaining ingredients and stir well, then bring to the boil, cover and simmer, stirring occasionally, for 15 minutes. Uncover and simmer for 5 minutes more until the sauce reduces down slightly.

Pickled cucumber sauce (serves 4)

4 rounded tablespoons vegan mayonnaise

2oz/50g pickled cucumber, finely chopped

1 tablespoon finely chopped fresh dill

1 tablespoon finely chopped fresh parsley

1 dessertspoon lemon juice

black pepper

Mix all the ingredients until well combined.

Apple sauce (serves 4)

12oz/350g eating apples, peeled, cored and finely chopped

1 tablespoon brown sugar

1 tablespoon lemon juice

1 tablespoon water

4 cloves

Put the ingredients in a saucepan and cook gently until the apple is soft. Remove the cloves and mash the apple smooth. Serve warm or cold.

Almond and mushroom sauce (serves 4)

1oz/25g ground almonds

¼oz/7g dried mushrooms

1 small onion, peeled and finely chopped

1 dessertspoon vegetable oil

10 fl.oz/300ml boiling water

2 tablespoons brandy

1 teaspoon brown sugar

black pepper

Soak the mushrooms in the boiling water for 30 minutes. Fry the onion in the oil until soft and add the mushrooms and soaking liquid, almonds, brandy and sugar. Season with black pepper and stir well. Bring to the boil and simmer for 5 minutes, then allow to cool slightly before blending smooth. Pour back into the cleaned pan and reheat while stirring.

Garlic sauce (serves 4)

4 garlic cloves, crushed

½oz/15g vegan margarine

½oz/15g cornflour

10 fl.oz/300ml vegetable stock

black pepper

Melt the margarine in a small pan, add the cornflour and mix until smooth. Take off the heat and stir in the garlic and stock. Season with black pepper and whisk to remove any lumps. Return to the heat, bring to the boil while stirring and keep stirring for a minute or two until the sauce thickens.

'Sour cream' (serves 8)

8oz/225g silken tofu, chopped

2 tablespoons lemon juice

2 dessertspoons soya milk

1 dessertspoon sunflower oil

black pepper

Put all the ingredients in a blender and blend smooth.

'Sour cream' with chives (serves 4)

4 rounded tablespoons vegan 'sour cream'

4 rounded tablespoons finely chopped fresh chives

Mix the chives with the 'sour cream' until well combined.

Horseradish sauce (serves 4)

4 rounded tablespoons vegan 'sour cream'

1 rounded tablespoon grated horseradish

½ teaspoon brown sugar

black pepper

Combine the ingredients well.

Vanilla sauce (serves 4)

10 fl.oz/300ml soya milk

1 teaspoon vanilla essence

½oz/15g brown sugar

½oz/15g cornflour

Mix the ingredients until smooth and transfer to a double boiler. Bring to the boil while stirring and continue stirring for a minute or so until the sauce thickens.

Chocolate sauce (serves 4)

Add

1oz/25g grated vegan chocolate

to the ingredients for vanilla sauce and proceed as above.

Coffee sauce (serves 4)

As for vanilla sauce, but add

1 dessertspoon instant coffee

SNACKS

Street vendors selling snacks are a familiar sight in many Eastern European towns and cities and food on offer is likely to include all kinds of little sweet and savoury pastries, pancakes and doughnuts, dumplings in sauces, roasted nuts and seeds and in season corn-on-the-cob and roasted chestnuts. Some foods such as buckwheat pancakes are traditionally eaten during the meatless weeks of Lent, especially in Poland. All of the following snacks are well suited for serving with salads as light meals and many of them make ideal buffet foods.

Pirozhki (makes approx. 20)

pastry

8oz/225g plain flour

1oz/25g vegan margarine, melted

1 teaspoon easy-blend yeast

pinch of salt

approx. 4 fl.oz/125ml soya milk, warmed

extra soya milk

filling

4oz/100g courgette, finely chopped

1oz/25g natural minced textured vegetable protein

1 small onion, peeled and finely chopped

1 garlic clove, crushed

4 fl.oz/125ml hot vegetable stock

2 rounded tablespoons finely chopped fresh parsley

¼ teaspoon paprika

2 fl.oz/50ml water

1 dessertspoon tomato purée

1 dessertspoon vegetable oil

black pepper

Soak the vegetable protein in the stock for 10 minutes. Fry the onion and garlic in the oil until softened, then add the vegetable protein and remaining stock, courgette, parsley and paprika. Dissolve the tomato purée in the water and add to the pan, season with black pepper and stir well. Bring to the boil and simmer uncovered, stirring occasionally, for about 5 minutes until the liquid has been absorbed. Remove from the heat and allow to cool.

Mix the flour, yeast and salt in a large bowl, stir in the melted margarine and add enough warmed soya milk to make a soft dough. Turn the dough out onto a floured board and knead it well. Return it to the bowl, cover and leave to rise for an hour in a warm place. Turn the dough out onto a floured board and knead again, then roll out to about ⅛ inch/3mm thick. Cut out 3 inch/8cm circles, gathering up and re-rolling the dough until it is all used up. Place about a dessertspoonful of filling on each circle and brush the edges with water. Fold the pastry over to enclose the filling and press the edges together with a fork. Make a slit in the top of each one and put them on a greased baking sheet. Leave in a warm place for 30 minutes to rise, then brush the tops with soya milk. Bake in a preheated oven at 180°C/350°F/Gas mark 4 for about 20 minutes until golden brown. Serve warm with a salad garnish.

Roasted aubergine and pepper dip (serves 4)

12oz/350g aubergine

6oz/175g red peppers

4oz/100g tomato, skinned and finely chopped

1 garlic clove, crushed

2 spring onions, trimmed and finely chopped

2 tablespoons finely chopped fresh parsley

1 dessertspoon lemon juice

1 dessertspoon red wine vinegar

1 dessertspoon olive oil

black pepper

extra olive oil

Cut the aubergine in half lengthways and brush the cut sides with olive oil. Place the aubergine and the red peppers on a baking tray under a hot grill, turning occasionally, until the skin blisters on the pepper and the aubergine is tender. Note: the pepper will be ready before the aubergine. Allow to cool, then peel the skin from the peppers and remove the membranes and seeds. Chop the flesh finely and put it in a bowl with the tomato, garlic, spring onions, parsley, lemon juice, vinegar and dessertspoonful of olive oil. Scoop the flesh from the aubergine into another bowl and mash until smooth. Add to the other ingredients and season with black pepper, mixing thoroughly. Spoon into a serving bowl, cover and chill.

Romanian aubergine cakes (makes 12)

12oz/350g aubergine
4oz/100g breadcrumbs
2oz/50g plain flour
1oz/25g vegan 'cheese', grated
4 spring onions, trimmed and finely chopped
2 garlic cloves, crushed
black pepper
vegetable oil

Make a few slits in the skin of the aubergine, put it on a baking sheet and bake it whole in a preheated oven at 180°C/350°F/Gas mark 4 for 25 minutes. Carefully peel off the skin and finely chop the flesh. Mix this thoroughly with the remaining ingredients except the oil, then take heaped dessertspoonfuls and roll into balls. Flatten each ball slightly and shallow fry them in hot vegetable oil in a non-stick frying pan for a few minutes on each side until golden. Drain on kitchen paper and serve hot with a salad.

White bean spread (serves 4/6)

1lb/450g cooked butter beans, skinned
2 garlic cloves, crushed
2 dessertspoons olive oil
2 dessertspoons lemon juice
2 dessertspoons water
black pepper
grated lemon zest

Mash the beans until smooth, then add the garlic, oil, lemon juice and water and season with black pepper. Mix well and transfer to a serving bowl. Garnish with lemon zest and use as a topping for warm crusty bread.

Czech potato pancakes (serves 4)

1lb/450g potatoes, peeled
1 onion, peeled and grated
2 garlic cloves, crushed
2 fl.oz/50ml soya milk
2oz/50g plain flour
1 dessertspoon dried parsley
black pepper
vegetable oil

Cut the potatoes into even-sized chunks and boil for 5 minutes. Drain and allow to cool, then grate them into a mixing bowl. Add the onion, garlic and parsley and season with black pepper. Combine the flour with the soya milk until smooth, add to the mixture and stir in well. Shallow fry rounded table-spoonfuls in hot vegetable oil, flattening each one out with the back of a spatula, for a few minutes on each side until browned. Drain on kitchen paper and serve warm, topped with 'sour cream' and with a salad garnish.

Fried cornmeal and 'cheese' balls (serves 4)

4oz/100g cornmeal
1oz/25g vegan 'cheese', grated
10 fl.oz/300ml vegetable stock
1 rounded dessertspoon vegan margarine
1 rounded teaspoon dried mixed herbs
black pepper
vegetable oil

Bring the stock to the boil, remove from the heat and add the cornmeal. Whisk until no lumps remain, then return to a very low heat and stir for a couple of minutes until thick. Take off the cooker and add the grated 'cheese', margarine and herbs and season with black pepper. Mix thoroughly, then take rounded dessertspoonfuls of the mixture and roll into balls. Shallow fry these in hot oil, turning occasionally, until golden brown. Drain on kitchen paper and serve hot with a salad garnish.

Toasted open sandwiches (serves 4)

4 large or 8 small slices of bread

vegan margarine

lettuce

pepper rings

tomato slices

sliced spring onions

2oz/50g natural minced textured vegetable protein

1 small onion, peeled and finely chopped

10 fl.oz/300ml vegetable stock

1 dessertspoon vegetable oil

1 rounded dessertspoon tomato purée

1 rounded tablespoon finely chopped fresh parsley

½ teaspoon paprika

black pepper

grated vegan white 'cheese'

Soak the vegetable protein in the stock for 15 minutes. Fry the chopped onion in the oil until soft, then add the vegetable protein and remaining stock, tomato purée, parsley and paprika. Season with black pepper and stir well. Bring to the boil and simmer for 5 minutes, stirring frequently. Meanwhile, toast the bread and spread one side of each slice with margarine. Put the bread on plates and top each slice with lettuce. Spoon the vegetable protein mixture over the lettuce, then sprinkle with grated 'cheese'. Garnish with pepper rings, tomato slices and spring onions.

Walnut- and 'cheese'-stuffed pancakes (serves 4)

pancakes

1½oz/40g self raising flour

½oz/15g soya flour

5 fl.oz/150ml soya milk

1 dessertspoon vegetable oil

vegan margarine

filling

2oz/50g vegan 'cream cheese'

1oz/25g walnuts, finely chopped

1oz/25g vegan white 'cheese', grated

1 small onion, peeled and finely chopped

1 garlic clove, crushed

1 dessertspoon vegetable oil

1 tablespoon finely chopped fresh parsley

1 tablespoon finely chopped fresh chives

black pepper

Mix the flours together, add the soya milk and oil and whisk thoroughly. Melt a little margarine in a small non-stick frying pan until hot. Add one table-spoonful of batter to the pan and swirl around to about 4 inches/10cm in diameter. Fry the pancake for a couple of minutes on each side until browned and repeat with the remaining batter to make 8 pancakes. Keep them warm while making the filling.

Fry the onion and garlic in the oil until soft. Remove from the heat and add the remaining filling ingredients. Mix well, then divide the filling equally between the pancakes. Fold or roll them up to enclose the filling and serve warm, topped with 'sour cream' or a sauce.

Bulgarian-style white beans (serves 4)

1lb/450g cooked haricot beans
6oz/175g tomatoes, skinned and chopped
1 onion, peeled and finely chopped
1 celery stick, trimmed and finely chopped
2 fl.oz/50ml water
1 rounded dessertspoon tomato purée
1 dessertspoon olive oil
1 rounded tablespoon finely chopped fresh mint
½ teaspoon paprika
black pepper
fresh mint leaves

Fry the onion and celery in the oil until soft. Add the tomatoes and cook until pulpy, then put in the beans, chopped mint and paprika. Dissolve the tomato purée in the water and add to the pan. Season with black pepper and simmer, stirring frequently, for 5 minutes. Transfer to a dish and garnish with fresh mint leaves. Serve with warm bread and a salad garnish.

Buckwheat pancakes (makes 12)

2oz/50g buckwheat flour
2oz/50g plain wholemeal flour
pinch of salt
1 teaspoon easy-blend yeast
9 fl.oz/250ml soya milk, warmed
vegetable oil

Mix the flours with the salt and yeast in a large bowl. Add the soya milk and whisk until smooth. Cover and leave in a warm place for 45 minutes until risen. Whisk the batter smooth again, then heat a small amount of vegetable oil in a non-stick frying pan. Drop tablespoonfuls of the batter into the pan, allowing enough room for spreading. Fry the pancakes for a few minutes on each side until golden, drain on kitchen paper and serve hot with a savoury topping.

Roasted baked peppers (serves 4)

4 red peppers, each approx. 5oz/150g

1 onion, peeled and finely chopped

1 garlic clove, crushed

1oz/25g vegan white 'cheese', grated

½oz/15g breadcrumbs

1 tablespoon olive oil

black pepper

vegan 'sour cream'

chopped walnuts

Cut the peppers in half lengthways and remove the stalks, membranes and seeds. Put them skin side up on a baking tray under a hot grill until the skins blister. Allow to cool slightly, then carefully remove the skins and put the pepper halves in a baking dish.

Soften the onion and garlic in the oil. Add the grated 'cheese' and the bread-crumbs and season with black pepper. Stir around on the heat for about 1 minute until well combined. Divide the mixture equally between the pepper halves and bake in a preheated oven at 180°C/350°F/Gas mark 4 for 12-15 minutes until browned. Top with 'sour cream' and chopped walnuts and serve with a salad garnish.

Uszka (serves 4)

pastry

4oz/100g plain flour

1 teaspoon easy-blend yeast

1 rounded dessertspoon dried parsley

pinch of salt

approx. 2½ fl.oz/75ml warm water

filling

2oz/50g vegan white 'cheese', grated

1oz/25g breadcrumbs

1 small onion, peeled and grated

1 garlic clove, crushed

1 dessertspoon vegetable oil

1 rounded tablespoon finely chopped fresh parsley

black pepper

Mix the flour with the yeast, parsley and salt and gradually add enough water to bind, then turn out onto a floured board and knead well. Return to the bowl, cover and leave in a warm place for 1 hour. Knead the dough again on a floured board, adding more flour if necessary until the dough loses its stickiness. Roll the dough out thinly to about ⅛ inch/3mm on a floured board and cut into 2 inch/5cm squares with a pastry cutter. Gather up and re-roll as necessary. Put the squares in a single layer on a floured piece of cling film and leave for 30 minutes.

Meanwhile fry the onion and garlic in the oil until soft, remove from the heat and add the remaining filling ingredients. Mix thoroughly, then dampen the edges of the pastry squares with water and place a teaspoonful of filling in the centre of each one. Fold the squares in half and press the edges together firmly to enclose the filling and make triangles.

Bring a large pan of water to the boil, add the triangles and boil them for 6 minutes. Remove with a slotted spoon and serve hot, topped with a sauce.

'Cheese' dumplings with 'cheese' and onion sauce (serves 4)

dumplings

4oz/100g plain flour

1oz/25g vegan margarine

1oz/25g vegan 'cheese', grated

1 teaspoon baking powder

1 teaspoon dried thyme

black pepper

approx. 3 tablespoons soya milk

20 fl.oz/600ml vegetable stock

sauce

1 small onion, peeled and finely chopped

1oz/25g vegan 'cheese', grated

1 dessertspoon vegetable oil

5 fl.oz/150ml soya milk

1 dessertspoon cornflour

black pepper

½oz/15g breadcrumbs

Sift the flour and baking powder into a mixing bowl and rub in the margarine. Stir in the 'cheese' and thyme and season with black pepper. Gradually add the soya milk until everything binds together. Take rounded teaspoonfuls of the dough and roll into tiny balls, then refrigerate these for a couple of hours. Bring the stock to the boil in a saucepan, add the dumplings and simmer for 10 minutes.

Fry the onion in the oil until soft. Dissolve the cornflour in the soya milk and add, together with the grated 'cheese'. Season with black pepper, bring to the boil while stirring and continue stirring for a minute or so until the sauce thickens.

Using a slotted spoon put the dumplings in a warmed ovenproof dish and pour the sauce evenly over the top. Sprinkle the breadcrumbs over the sauce and place the dish under a hot grill for a couple of minutes until the crumbs are golden. Serve hot with a salad garnish.

Runzas (makes approx. 15)

pastry

6oz/175g plain flour

1 teaspoon easy-blend yeast

pinch of salt

1 tablespoon vegetable oil

approx. 2½ fl.oz/65ml warm water

soya milk

filling

1oz/25g natural minced textured vegetable protein

1oz/25g vegan white 'cheese', grated

1 tablespoon sauerkraut

2 spring onions, trimmed and finely chopped

1 garlic clove, crushed

4 fl.oz/125ml hot vegetable stock

1 dessertspoon vegetable oil

1 tablespoon finely chopped fresh parsley

1 dessertspoon tomato purée

¼ teaspoon caraway seed

black pepper

Mix the flour with the yeast and salt, stir in the oil and gradually add the warm water until a soft dough forms. Knead the dough well, return to the bowl, cover and leave in a warm place for 1 hour.

Meanwhile soak the vegetable protein in the hot stock for 15 minutes. Fry the spring onions and garlic in the oil until soft, then add the vegetable protein and remaining filling ingredients apart from the 'cheese'. Raise the heat and stir around for 2 minutes before allowing to cool.

Knead the dough again and roll it out on a floured board to about ⅛ inch/3mm thick. Cut the dough into 2½ inch/6cm squares with a pastry cutter, gathering up and re-rolling as necessary. Spread the squares on a flat surface and divide the filling equally between them, putting it in the middle. Sprinkle the grated 'cheese' on top and dampen the pastry edges with water. Fold the pastry over to enclose the filling and make small triangles. Press the edges together to join and put them on a greased baking sheet. Make a slit in the top of each triangle and leave them in a warm place for 30 minutes. Brush them with soya milk and bake in a preheated oven at 180°C/350°F/Gas mark 4 for 18-20 minutes until golden. Serve warm with a salad garnish.

Walnut- and mushroom-stuffed pastries (makes 6)

12 9 x 5inch/23x13cm sheets of filo pastry

vegetable oil

poppy seeds

filling

4oz/100g vegan 'cream cheese'

2oz/50g walnuts, grated

2oz/50g breadcrumbs

½oz/15g dried mushrooms

3 fl.oz/75ml boiling water

1 onion, peeled and finely chopped

1 garlic clove, crushed

1 dessertspoon vegetable oil

black pepper

Soak the mushrooms in the boiling water for 30 minutes. Soften the onion and garlic in the oil, add the mushrooms and soaking liquid and bring to the boil. Simmer for a couple of minutes until the liquid has been absorbed, then remove from the heat, add the remaining filling ingredients and mix well. Spread out 6 of the filo sheets and brush lightly with oil, then put another sheet of filo on top of each one. Divide the filling equally between the 6 oblongs, placing it at one end only. Fold the long edges over to enclose the sides of the filling, then fold each pastry up to make 6 small oblongs. Put them on an oiled baking sheet, brush with oil and sprinkle with poppy seeds. Bake in a preheated oven at 180°C/350°F/Gas mark 4 for 20-25 minutes until golden brown. Serve warm, topped with 'sour cream' and with a salad garnish.

GRAINS

A variety of grains are enjoyed throughout Eastern Europe and as well as being used in savoury dishes some grains such as millet and buckwheat are also made into porridge-type dishes which are eaten for breakfast. Buckwheat is especially popular in Poland and is served with all kinds of food. In Romania and Bulgaria rice dishes are a favourite, especially those containing spinach, courgettes or tomatoes. Maize, a staple crop in Romania, is traditionally ground and made into a polenta-style dish called mamaliga, eaten with stews and casseroles.

Savoury fruit and vegetable rice (serves 4)

8oz/225g long grain rice

4oz/100g carrot, scraped and finely chopped

4oz/100g green pepper, chopped

4oz/100g red pepper, chopped

2oz/50g pitted prunes, finely chopped

2oz/50g dried apricots, finely chopped

2 celery sticks, trimmed and finely chopped

1 onion, peeled and chopped

2 garlic cloves, crushed

1 red chilli, deseeded and finely chopped

1 tablespoon vegetable oil

few strands of saffron

4 cloves

black pepper

4 tablespoons fresh apple juice

2 tablespoons lemon juice

20 fl.oz/600ml vegetable stock

plain soya yoghurt

fresh dill

cucumber slices

quartered cherry tomatoes

Mix the apple juice with the lemon juice and add the prunes and apricots. Cover and leave to soak for 2 hours. Fry the carrot, celery, onion, garlic and chilli in the oil for 5 minutes. Add the rice, green and red pepper, soaked fruit, saffron, cloves and stock and season with black pepper. Stir well and bring to the boil, then cover and simmer gently until the liquid has been absorbed. Transfer to a serving dish and garnish with a swirl of yoghurt and some fresh dill, cucumber slices and cherry tomatoes.

Millet with mushrooms (serves 4)

8oz/225g millet

8oz/225g mushrooms, wiped and sliced

½oz/15g dried mushrooms

1 onion, peeled and finely chopped

2 garlic cloves, crushed

4 fl.oz/125ml boiling water

20 fl.oz/600ml vegetable stock

1 tablespoon vegetable oil

black pepper

chopped walnuts

finely chopped fresh parsley

Soak the dried mushrooms in the boiling water for 30 minutes. Heat the oil and fry the onion and garlic for 3 minutes. Add the millet and fresh mushrooms and stir around for 1 minute, then put in the dried mushrooms and remaining soaking liquid together with the vegetable stock. Season with black pepper and stir well. Bring to the boil, cover and simmer gently for about 20 minutes until the liquid has been absorbed. Spoon into a dish and garnish with chopped walnuts and parsley.

Rice with spinach, courgettes and leeks (serves 4)

1lb/450g fresh spinach, finely shredded

12oz/350g courgettes, chopped

12oz/350g leeks, trimmed and finely sliced

8oz/225g long grain rice

2 garlic cloves, crushed

1 tablespoon vegetable oil

2 bay leaves

black pepper

20 fl.oz/600ml vegetable stock

chopped walnuts

Heat the oil in a large pan and fry the leek and garlic for 3 minutes. Put in the spinach and cook while stirring for 3 minutes more. Add the courgette, rice, bay leaves and stock and season with black pepper. Stir well and bring to the boil, then cover and simmer very gently until the liquid has been absorbed. Sprinkle with chopped walnuts before serving.

Braised cabbage with bulgar wheat (serves 4)

8oz/225g bulgar wheat

6oz/175g white cabbage, finely shredded

1 small onion, peeled and finely chopped

4oz/100g tomato, skinned and chopped

1 tablespoon vegetable oil

2 rounded tablespoons sauerkraut

16 fl.oz/475ml hot vegetable stock

2 fl.oz/50ml tomato juice

2 tablespoons finely chopped fresh parsley

1 teaspoon paprika

black pepper

fresh parsley

Fry the cabbage and onion in the oil for 5 minutes, then add the tomato, tomato juice and paprika and simmer for 15 minutes, stirring occasionally, until done. Meanwhile soak the bulgar wheat in the hot vegetable stock for 15 minutes. Add this to the pan with the sauerkraut and chopped parsley, season with black pepper and cook for another couple of minutes, stirring constantly until well combined. Serve garnished with fresh parsley.

Buckwheat with fried onions (serves 4)

8oz/225g roasted buckwheat

8oz/225g onion, peeled and finely sliced

2 dessertspoons vegetable oil

8 fl.oz/225ml vegetable stock

pinch of grated nutmeg

black pepper

plain soya yoghurt

chopped walnuts

Soak the buckwheat in water for 3 minutes, transfer to a fine sieve and steam over a pan of boiling water for 5 minutes. Meanwhile fry the onion in the oil until soft. Add the buckwheat, vegetable stock and nutmeg and season with black pepper. Stir well and bring to the boil, then simmer while stirring for 3 minutes until the liquid has been absorbed. Garnish with plain yoghurt and walnuts.

Barley with mixed beans (serves 4)

8oz/225g pot barley

4oz/100g green beans, topped, tailed and cut into ½ inch/1cm lengths

4oz/100g cooked mixed beans

1 onion, peeled and finely chopped

1 dessertspoon vegetable oil

1 rounded tablespoon finely chopped fresh marjoram

1 bay leaf

black pepper

1 tablespoon lemon juice

grated vegan 'cheese'

Soak the barley in boiling water for 1 hour, drain and bring to the boil in fresh water. Cover and simmer for 30 minutes, then strain the cooking liquid off into a measuring jug. Soften the onion in the oil. Add the green beans, barley, marjoram and bay leaf and season with black pepper. Make the cooking liquid up to 12 fl.oz/350ml with water if necessary and add to the pan. Stir well and bring to the boil, cover and simmer, stirring occasionally, for 10 minutes. Add the mixed beans and cook for a couple of minutes more until the liquid has been absorbed and the barley is done. Stir in the lemon juice, transfer to a serving dish and sprinkle with grated 'cheese'.

Tomato and courgette rice (serves 4)

8oz/225g long grain rice

8oz/225g tomatoes, skinned and chopped

8oz/225g courgette, chopped

1 onion, peeled and finely chopped

1 garlic clove, crushed

1 small red chilli, finely chopped

1 dessertspoon vegetable oil

1 rounded tablespoon fresh thyme

1 tablespoon tomato purée

1 tablespoon red wine vinegar

1 teaspoon paprika

black pepper

20 fl.oz/600ml vegetable stock

chopped fresh parsley

Fry the onion, garlic and chilli in the oil for 3 minutes. Add the tomatoes and cook until pulpy, then the remaining ingredients apart from the parsley and stir well. Bring to the boil, cover and simmer gently until the liquid has been absorbed and the rice is cooked. Serve garnished with chopped parsley.

Bulgar wheat with leeks and prunes (serves 4)

12oz/350g leeks, trimmed and finely sliced

8oz/225g bulgar wheat

2oz/50g pitted prunes, chopped

1 tablespoon vegetable oil

1 tablespoon lemon juice

black pepper

20 fl.oz/600ml vegetable stock

vegan 'sour cream'

Fry the leeks in the oil for 5 minutes, stirring frequently. Add the lemon juice, prunes and a quarter of the stock, bring to the boil, cover and simmer for 5 minutes. Put in the remaining stock and the bulgar wheat and season with black pepper. Stir well and bring back to the boil. Cover and simmer very gently until the liquid has been absorbed. Garnish with 'sour cream' when serving.

Mamaliga (serves 4)

4oz/100g cornmeal

20 fl.oz/600ml vegetable stock

olive oil

Bring the stock to the boil, then remove from the heat and gradually add the cornmeal, whisking between additions until smooth. Return to a low heat and cook, stirring occasionally, for about 10 minutes until the mixture is thick. Spoon into a lined 8 inch/20cm round tin and flatten with the back of a wet spoon. Cover and refrigerate for a couple of hours until firm. Invert the mamaliga onto a plate and cut into 8 wedges. Carefully transfer these to an oiled baking dish and brush the tops with olive oil. Bake in a preheated oven at 180°C/350°F/Gas mark 4 for 20 minutes, then turn the wedges over, brush them with oil and put back in the oven for 20 minutes more. Serve warm with stews and casseroles.

Steamed millet with vegetables (serves 4)

8oz/225g millet

8oz/225g prepared vegetables (e.g. carrot, peppers, broccoli, mushrooms), finely chopped

1 onion, peeled and finely chopped

1 garlic clove, crushed

1 tablespoon vegetable oil

6 fl.oz/175ml vegetable stock

1 tablespoon tomato purée

1 tablespoon lemon juice

1 bay leaf

½ teaspoon paprika

black pepper

1 tomato, cut into wedges

finely chopped fresh parsley

Soak the millet in boiling water for 15 minutes. Drain and steam in a fine sieve over a pan of boiling water for 25-30 minutes until done, stirring occasionally to ensure even cooking.

Meanwhile fry all the vegetables in the oil for 5 minutes. Stir in the stock, tomato purée, lemon juice, bay leaf and paprika, season with black pepper and bring to the boil. Cover and simmer gently for about 20 minutes until tender. Remove from the heat and add the steamed millet. Mix thoroughly, then spoon into a dish, arrange the tomato wedges around the edge and garnish with chopped parsley.

BREADS

A meal without bread is not considered to be a proper meal in Eastern European countries and whether it is used to mop up soups or stews or to accompany other main courses or snacks, some type of bread is eaten with every meal. The bread favoured by each of the countries is largely determined by the type of grain grown there. As well as various breads made from wheat those made with rye are very popular in the northern areas, while breads that include cornmeal and chickpea flour are found in the southern parts. A wide variety of sweet breads are also enjoyed, while doughnuts made with potato, split open and filled with savoury fillings are popular snacks sold by street vendors. All home-made breads are best eaten on the day of baking, but can be frozen.

Dark rye bread

8oz/225g rye flour

8oz/225g strong wholemeal bread flour

1 dessertspoon easy-blend yeast

½ teaspoon salt

1oz/25g vegan margarine

2 rounded tablespoons molasses

1 rounded tablespoon vegan 'sour cream'

1 teaspoon caraway seeds

approx. 7 fl.oz/200ml warm water

Mix the rye and wholemeal flours with the yeast, salt and caraway seeds. Melt the margarine and molasses in a small pan and add, together with the 'sour cream'. Mix well, then gradually add the water until a stiff dough forms. Turn out onto a floured board and knead for 5 minutes. Put the dough in a greased 8 inch/20cm loaf tin, gently pressing it out to fill the tin, and leave in a warm place for 1 hour until risen, then bake in a preheated oven at 200°C/400°F/Gas mark 6 for about 25 minutes until hollow sounding when tapped underneath. Allow to cool on a wire rack before cutting into thin slices.

Light rye bread

8oz/225g rye flour

8oz/225g strong white bread flour

1 dessertspoon easy-blend yeast

½ teaspoon salt

1oz/25g vegan margarine, melted

1 teaspoon caraway seeds

approx. 10 fl.oz/300ml warm water

Put the rye flour, white flour, yeast, salt and caraway seeds into a bowl and mix. Stir in the melted margarine, then gradually add the water until a soft dough forms. Turn out onto a floured board and knead the dough for 5 minutes. Return to the bowl, cover and leave in a warm place for 1 hour to rise. Knead the dough again and shape it into a 6 inch/15cm round. Transfer to a greased baking tray and leave in a warm place for 30 minutes. Bake in a preheated oven at 200°C/400°F/Gas mark 6 for about 25 minutes until browned. Slide onto a wire rack to cool.

Hungarian coffee bread

dough

12oz/350g plain flour

1oz/25g vegan margarine, melted

1oz/25g brown sugar

1 rounded teaspoon easy-blend yeast

1 rounded teaspoon instant coffee

6 fl.oz/175ml soya milk, warmed

dipping mixture

1½oz/40g walnuts, finely chopped

½oz/15g brown sugar

½ teaspoon ground cinnamon

½oz/15g vegan margarine, melted

Combine the flour with the yeast and sugar, add the melted margarine and mix well. Dissolve the coffee in the warmed soya milk, add and stir until a soft dough forms. Turn out onto a floured board and knead well. Return to the bowl, cover and leave in a warm place for 1 hour until risen. Knead the dough again on a floured board and divide it into 20 equal portions. Roll each portion into a ball.

Mix the walnuts with the sugar and cinnamon in a bowl. Dip each ball in the melted margarine and then in the walnut mixture until coated and put them in an 8 inch/20cm greased loaf tin, filling the space so that no gaps remain. Cover and leave in a warm place for 45 minutes to rise. Cover with foil and bake in a preheated oven at 200°C/400°F/Gas mark 6 for 20 minutes, then take off the foil and bake for 10 minutes more until golden brown. Leave to cool on a wire rack before cutting into slices.

Cornbread

4oz/100g cornmeal

4oz/100g plain flour

1oz/25g vegan 'cheese', grated

1 rounded teaspoon baking powder

½ teaspoon salt

2 tablespoons vegetable oil

8 fl.oz/225ml soya milk

Sift the flour, baking powder and salt into a mixing bowl. Stir in the cornmeal and oil, add the grated 'cheese' and then the soya milk and mix thoroughly, Spoon the dough into a 7 inch/18cm diameter greased baking tin. Level the top and bake in a preheated oven at 180°C/350°F/Gas mark 4 for about 25 minutes until golden. Turn out onto a wire rack and allow to cool slightly before cutting into slices or wedges. Serve warm.

Potato doughnuts (makes 10)

9oz/250g plain flour

6oz/175g potato, peeled and cut into large chunks

1 rounded teaspoon easy-blend yeast

½ teaspoon salt

approx. 5 fl.oz/150ml warm water

vegetable oil

Boil the potato for 10 minutes, drain and allow to cool. Grate the potato and mix with the flour, yeast and salt, then gradually add the water until a stiff dough forms. Knead this on a floured board, then return to the bowl, cover and leave in a warm place for 45 minutes. Knead the dough again and divide it into 10 equal portions. Roll each one into a ball and put these on an oiled baking sheet in a warm place for 30 minutes. Flatten the balls slightly, then shallow fry them in hot vegetable oil for a few minutes on each side until golden. Drain on kitchen paper and serve warm.

Poppy seed and walnut rolls (makes 8)

8oz/225g plain wholemeal flour

1 rounded teaspoon easy-blend yeast

½ teaspoon salt

1 tablespoon vegetable oil

1 rounded tablespoon poppy seeds

approx. 5 fl.oz/150ml soya milk, warmed

1½oz/40g walnuts, finely chopped

extra soya milk

extra poppy seeds

Mix the flour with the salt, yeast and tablespoonful of poppy seeds, add the oil and combine well. Gradually add the warmed soya milk until a soft dough forms. Turn out onto a floured board and knead. Return to the bowl, cover and leave in a warm place for 1 hour until risen. Knead the dough again and roll it out on a floured board into a 9 inch/23cm square. Sprinkle the chopped walnuts evenly over the dough and roll it up like a Swiss roll. Dampen the edge with soya milk and press to join. Cut the roll into 8 equal slices and put these flat on a greased baking sheet. Leave in a warm place for 45 minutes to rise, then brush the tops with soya milk and sprinkle with poppy seeds. Bake in a preheated oven at 200°C/400°F/Gas mark 6 for 12-15 minutes until browned.

Bulgarian 'cheese'-stuffed rolls (makes 8)

8oz/225g plain flour

1 dessertspoon easy-blend yeast

½ teaspoon salt

1 tablespoon vegetable oil

approx. 4½ fl.oz/137ml warm water

2oz/50g vegan white 'cheese', grated

soya milk

Combine the flour, salt and yeast in a mixing bowl. Stir in the oil, then gradually add the water until a soft dough forms. Knead the dough well, return it to the bowl, cover and leave in a warm place for 1 hour to rise. Knead the dough again on a floured board and divide into 8 equal pices. Form each piece of dough into a cup shape and fill them with some of the grated 'cheese'. Dampen the edges of the dough with water and press together to seal and enclose the 'cheese'. Reshape the dough into balls, put them on a greased baking sheet and leave in a warm place for 30 minutes. Brush with soya milk and bake in a preheated oven at 200°C/400°F/Gas mark 6 for 15-18 minutes until golden brown. Allow to cool slightly before serving.

Hungarian potato plait

8oz/225g strong white bread flour

4oz/100g potato, peeled and chopped

1 tablespoon vegetable oil

1 teaspoon easy-blend yeast

½ teaspoon salt

½ teaspoon fennel seed

approx. 4 fl.oz/125ml warm water

Cook the potato, drain and dry off over a low heat. Mash and allow to cool. Mix the flour with the yeast, salt and fennel seed, stir in the oil and potato and then gradually add the water until a soft dough forms. Turn out onto a floured board and knead well. Return to the bowl, cover and leave to rise in a warm place for 1 hour. Knead the dough again and divide into 3 equal pieces. Shape each piece into a roll of about 8 inches/20cm long. Plait the rolls together and place on a greased baking sheet. Leave in a warm place for 30 minutes, then bake in a preheated oven at 200°C/400°F/Gas mark 6 for 18-20 minutes until browned. Slide onto a wire rack to cool before cutting into slices.

Chickpea buns

8oz/225g plain flour

4oz/100g chickpea flour

1 dessertspoon easy-blend yeast

½ teaspoon salt

2 tablespoons vegetable oil

approx. 6 fl.oz/175ml warm water

soya milk

Mix the two flours, yeast and salt. Stir in the oil and gradually add the warm water until a stiff dough forms. Knead this well, return it to the bowl and leave in a warm place for 1 hour. Knead the dough again and divide it into 10 equal pieces. Roll these into balls and arrange 7 of them in a circle on a greased baking sheet. Put the other 3 balls in the centre and gently squeeze the whole circle together so that all the balls are touching. Leave in a warm place for 30 minutes to rise, then brush with soya milk. Bake in a preheated oven at 200°C/400°F/Gas mark 6 for 12-15 minutes until golden. Put on a wire rack to cool before breaking into the individual buns.

'Milk' bread with raisins

12oz/350g plain wholemeal flour

1 dessertspoon easy-blend yeast

½ teaspoon salt

1 tablespoon sunflower oil

2oz/50g raisins, chopped

9 fl.oz/250ml soya milk

extra soya milk

Bring the raisins and soya milk to the boil, simmer for 2 minutes, then remove from the heat and leave to cool for 20 minutes.

Mix the flour with the salt and yeast in a large bowl. Stir in the oil, then add the raisin and 'milk' mixture and combine thoroughly. Turn the dough out onto a floured board and knead well. Return to the bowl, cover and leave to rise for an hour in a warm place. Knead the dough again on a floured board and shape it to fit a greased 8 inch/20cm loaf tin. Keep in a warm place for 30 minutes, then brush the top with soya milk and bake in a preheated oven at 200°C/400°F/Gas mark 6 for about 20 minutes until golden brown. Turn out onto a wire rack and allow to cool before cutting into slices.

SALADS

Salads made with a combination of ingredients as well as those made from a single vegetable are popular in all of the countries. Cabbage, tomato, cucumber, boiled potato, beetroot and mushrooms are all typical vegetables that would be used singly and these are usually chopped or shredded and simply tossed in an oil and vinegar and lemon juice dressing. Cold cooked beans and chickpeas are also served in this way. Salads are commonly used to accompany main courses or savoury snacks or are served as starters or buffet dishes.

Bulgarian shopska salad (serves 4)

8oz/225g tomatoes

8oz/225g cucumber

8oz/225g green pepper

1 small red chilli, deseeded and finely chopped

1 small onion, peeled and finely chopped

2oz/50g vegan white 'cheese', grated

2 rounded tablespoons finely chopped fresh parsley

1 tablespoon olive oil

1 dessertspoon white wine vinegar

1 teaspoon lemon juice

black pepper

Finely dice the tomatoes, cucumber and green pepper and put them in a mixing bowl with the chilli, onion and parsley. Combine the oil with the vinegar and the lemon juice and add, season with black pepper and toss thoroughly. Transfer to a serving bowl and sprinkle with the grated 'cheese'.

Courgettes with yoghurt (serves 4)

1¼lb/550g courgettes, halved lengthways and sliced

4 rounded tablespoons plain soya yoghurt

2 garlic cloves, crushed

1 tablespoon finely chopped fresh dill

black pepper

sprig of fresh dill

Steam the courgettes to soften them slightly, then put them in a bowl in the fridge until cold. Mix the yoghurt with the garlic and chopped dill and season with black pepper. Add to the courgettes and combine well. Spoon into a dish and garnish with a sprig of fresh dill.

Celeriac and apple salad (serves 4)

1lb/450g celeriac, peeled and cut into large chunks

2 red-skinned eating apples, cored

1 tablespoon vegetable oil

1 dessertspoon lemon juice

1 teaspoon white wine vinegar

extra lemon juice

1 tablespoon finely chopped fresh chives

black pepper

vegan 'sour cream'

extra chopped fresh chives

Put the celeriac in a pan and cover with water, add a dash of lemon juice and boil for 5 minutes. Drain and rinse under cold running water, then grate into a bowl. Finely chop one of the apples and add to the celeriac. Mix the oil with the dessertspoonful of lemon juice and the vinegar and add to the salad with the tablespoon of chives. Season with black pepper and toss well. Spoon the salad into a serving bowl. Cut the other apple into slices, arrange these around the edge and garnish the salad with 'sour cream' and chopped chives.

Sweet pepper salad (serves 4)

1lb/450g mixed peppers, chopped

6oz/175g tomatoes, skinned and chopped

1 tablespoon sunflower oil

2 rounded tablespoons vegan mayonnaise

1 garlic clove, crushed

black pepper

chopped walnuts

shredded lettuce leaves

Cook the peppers and tomatoes in the oil for about 15 minutes, stirring frequently, until the mixture is thick and the peppers are soft. Allow to cool, then refrigerate until cold. Stir the mayonnaise and garlic into the cold pepper mixture and season with black pepper. Arrange some shredded lettuce on a serving plate and pile the salad on top. Garnish with chopped walnuts.

Mixed bean and corn salad (serves 4)

8oz/225g mixed cooked beans

8oz/225g sweetcorn kernels

2oz/50g gherkins, finely chopped

2oz/50g tomato, skinned and finely chopped

4 spring onions, trimmed and finely sliced

1 garlic clove, crushed

1 rounded tablespoon finely chopped fresh dill

1 tablespoon olive oil

1 dessertspoon lemon juice

black pepper

Blanch the sweetcorn kernels, drain and rinse under cold running water and put in a mixing bowl with the beans, gherkins, spring onions and dill. Combine the olive oil with the lemon juice, garlic and tomato and season with black pepper. Add to the salad, toss thoroughly and spoon into a serving bowl.

Beetroot and horseradish salad (serves 4)

1lb/450g cooked beetroot, finely chopped

2 tablespoons grated horseradish

1 tablespoon red wine vinegar

1 rounded teaspoon brown sugar

black pepper

Mix all the ingredients until well combined, then transfer to a dish, cover and chill before serving.

Carrot and chickpea salad (serves 4)

12oz/350g carrots, scraped and cut into ½ inch/1cm long
   matchsticks

6oz/175g cooked chickpeas

3 spring onions, trimmed and finely chopped

3 gherkins, finely chopped

1 garlic clove, crushed

1 tablespoon finely chopped fresh dill

1 dessertspoon vegetable oil

1 tablespoon lemon juice

black pepper

Steam the carrots until just tender, then rinse in cold water to refresh. Drain
and put in a large bowl with the chickpeas, spring onions, gherkins, garlic and
dill. Mix the lemon juice with the oil and add. Season with black pepper and
toss well. Put in a serving bowl, cover and chill.

Potato salad with 'sour cream' and chives
(serves 4)

1½lb/675g potatoes, peeled

2 rounded tablespoons vegan 'sour cream'

2 rounded tablespoons finely chopped fresh chives

6 spring onions, trimmed and finely sliced

1 garlic clove, crushed

black pepper

extra chopped fresh chives

Boil or steam the potatoes, drain and rinse under cold water. Allow to cool,
then dice them and put them in a bowl with the spring onions. Mix the 'sour
cream' with the chives and garlic and season with black pepper. Add to the
potatoes and toss well before transferring the salad to a serving dish and
garnishing it with chopped chives.

Sauerkraut and vegetables salad (serves 4)

4oz/100g sauerkraut

2oz/50g mushrooms, wiped and chopped

2oz/50g sweetcorn kernels

2oz/50g green beans, topped, tailed and cut into ½ inch/1cm lengths

2oz/50g cauliflower, cut into tiny florets

2oz/50g red pepper, finely chopped

2oz/50g green pepper, finely chopped

4 spring onions, trimmed and finely sliced

1 garlic clove, crushed

1 tablespoon finely chopped fresh dill

1 tablespoon finely chopped fresh parsley

2 rounded tablespoons vegan mayonnaise

2 dessertspoons lemon juice

black pepper

chopped gherkins

tomato wedges

Steam the sweetcorn kernels, green beans and cauliflower to soften slightly. Rinse under cold running water and combine with the sauerkraut, mushrooms, red and green peppers, spring onions, garlic, dill and parsley. Mix the lemon juice with the mayonnaise and add, season with black pepper and toss. Spoon into a bowl, arrange the tomato wedges around the edge and garnish with chopped gherkins.

Beetroot and orange salad (serves 4)

1lb/450g cooked beetroot, finely chopped

1 orange

1 dessertspoon vegetable oil

1 dessertspoon white wine vinegar

½ teaspoon caraway seeds

black pepper

vegan 'sour cream'

Peel the orange and grate a little of the peel for garnish. Remove the pith, membranes and seeds and chop the segments. Strain off and keep the juice. Put the chopped orange and beetroot in a mixing bowl. Mix the oil with 2 dessert-spoonfuls of the orange juice, the vinegar and the caraway seeds and season with black pepper. Add the dressing to the salad and toss thoroughly, then put in a serving bowl and garnish with 'sour cream' and grated orange peel.

Pickled cucumber salad (serves 4)

8oz/225g cucumber, finely chopped

4oz/100g pickled cucumber, finely chopped

2oz/50g walnuts, chopped

1 garlic clove, crushed

1 rounded tablespoon finely chopped fresh dill

8 rounded tablespoons plain soya yoghurt

1 tablespoon white wine vinegar

black pepper

shredded lettuce

extra fresh dill

Combine the cucumbers, walnuts, garlic, chopped dill, yoghurt and vinegar in a large bowl and season with black pepper. Arrange some shredded lettuce on a serving plate and pile the salad on top. Garnish with fresh dill.

Courgette and tomato salad (serves 4)

1lb/450g courgette, chopped

8oz/225g tomatoes, skinned and finely chopped

1 small onion, peeled and finely chopped

1 tablespoon vegetable oil

1 garlic clove, crushed

1 tablespoon finely chopped fresh marjoram

1 tablespoon white wine vinegar

black pepper

Heat the oil in a pan and fry the onion for 2 minutes. Add the courgette and continue frying until it is softened. Remove from the heat, add the remaining ingredients and mix well. Spoon into a bowl and cover and chill before serving.

Potato and cucumber salad (serves 4)

1¼lb/550g potatoes, peeled

4oz/100g cucumber, finely chopped

2oz/50g pickled cucumber, finely chopped

4 spring onions, trimmed and finely sliced

1 rounded tablespoon finely chopped fresh parsley

1 rounded tablespoon finely chopped fresh dill

black pepper

2 rounded tablespoons vegan mayonnaise

2 dessertspoons lemon juice

cucumber slices

Boil or steam the potatoes and rinse them under cold running water, then dice them and refrigerate until cold. Add the chopped cucumbers, spring onions, parsley and dill and season with black pepper. Combine the lemon juice with the mayonnaise, and toss well. Arrange cucumber slices around the edge of the salad bowl before serving.

Summer vegetable salad (serves 4)

12oz/350g aubergine

4oz/100g sweetcorn kernels

4oz/100g red pepper, finely chopped

4oz/100g green pepper, finely chopped

4 spring onions, trimmed and finely sliced

1 garlic clove, crushed

1 rounded tablespoon finely chopped fresh marjoram

1 tablespoon olive oil

1 teaspoon lemon juice

1 teaspoon red wine vinegar

black pepper

plain soya yoghurt

chopped gherkins

Make a few slits in the skin of the aubergine and bake it whole in a preheated oven at 180°C/350°F/Gas mark 4 for about 30-35 minutes until just tender. Allow to cool, carefully remove the skin, chop the flesh and put this in the fridge for a couple of hours in a covered dish. Blanch the sweetcorn, then rinse under cold running water. Drain well and place in a mixing bowl with the red and green peppers, spring onions, garlic and marjoram. Add the aubergine and combine well. Mix the olive oil with the lemon juice and vinegar and season with black pepper, pour over the salad and toss thoroughly. Spoon into a bowl and garnish with plain yoghurt and chopped gherkins.

Beetroot, sauerkraut and apple salad
(serves 4)

8oz/225g raw beetroot, peeled and grated

6oz/175g sauerkraut

1 eating apple, cored and grated

4 fl.oz/125ml fresh apple juice

1 tablespoon red wine vinegar

½ teaspoon dill seed

black pepper

Put the beetroot, apple juice and dill seed in a saucepan and bring to the boil. Simmer uncovered for about 8 minutes until the liquid has been absorbed. Put the beetroot in a covered bowl in the fridge, and when cold add the remaining ingredients and mix well.

DESSERTS

The orchards of Eastern Europe produce vast crops of apples, pears, plums, apricots and cherries and these are often combined with seasonal soft fruits to make fresh or stewed fruit salads. Summer fruits are also dried or bottled for use during the winter months. A traditional Hungarian purée called lekvar, which is made from dried apricots or prunes, is widely used as a topping or a filling for various pastries and pancakes. In fact, the humble pancake is by far the most popular dessert in many of the countries and they are also filled with jam or stewed apples, or folded and served flambé in fruit-flavoured liqueurs. Strudels made with filo pastry and filled with fresh or dried fruits or ground nuts are another favourite, especially in the south of the region.

Winter fruit compote (serves 6)

12oz/350g dried fruits (e.g. apples, apricots, peaches, pears, prunes)

6 cloves

2 inch/5cm stick of cinnamon

8 fl.oz/225ml fresh apple juice

8 fl.oz/225ml water

Put all the ingredients in a saucepan, cover and leave to soak for 1 hour. Bring to the boil, cover and simmer for about 15 minutes until the fruit is plump. Allow to cool, then refrigerate until cold. Remove the cinnamon stick and cloves and serve the fruit topped with yoghurt.

Baked prunes with 'sour cream' (serves 4)

8oz/225g pitted prunes

4 rounded tablespoons vegan 'sour cream'

1oz/25g breadcrumbs

1 rounded teaspoon vegan margarine

1 teaspoon brown sugar

½ teaspoon ground cinnamon

Put the prunes in a pan and cover with water. Bring to the boil, cover and simmer until plump. Drain and allow to cool, then chop them and divide them between 4 ovenproof ramekin dishes. Melt the margarine in a small pan, remove from the heat and stir in the breadcrumbs, sugar and cinnamon. Spoon 1 tablespoonful of 'sour cream' into each of the dishes of prunes and sprinkle the breadcrumb mixture evenly over the top. Bake in a preheated oven at 180°C/350°F/Gas mark 4 for 15 minutes until golden brown. Serve warm.

Coffee and hazelnut pots (serves 4)

16 fl.oz/475ml soya milk

1½oz/40g brown sugar

1 tablespoon coffee granules

2 rounded tablespoons cornflour

1 teaspoon vanilla essence

toasted chopped hazelnuts

Mix the sugar, coffee, cornflour and vanilla with the soya milk until smooth and pour into a double boiler. Bring to the boil while stirring and continue stirring for a minute or so until the mixture thickens. Divide it equally between four 3 inch/8cm ramekin dishes, cover and put in the fridge to get cold. Sprinkle with toasted chopped hazelnuts when serving.

Slovakian rice and apple pudding (serves 4)

4oz/100g long grain rice

10 fl.oz/300ml water

10 fl.oz/300ml soya milk

1 tablespoon finely grated lemon peel

1oz/25g brown sugar

1oz/25g sultanas

2 tablespoons fresh apple juice

1 eating apple, peeled, cored and thinly sliced

ground cinnamon

Soak the sultanas in the apple juice for 30 minutes to soften. Bring the rice and water to the boil, cover and simmer gently until the water has been absorbed. Remove from the heat and stir in the soya milk, lemon peel, sugar and the soaked sultanas and remaining juice. Return to the heat, bring back to the boil and simmer for 3 minutes. Ladle half of the mixture into a deep 7 inch/18cm diameter ovenproof dish and arrange the apple slices on top. Spoon the remaining rice mixture over the apples and sprinkle with ground cinnamon. Cover tightly with foil and bake in a preheated oven at 180°C/350°F/Gas mark 4 for 25 minutes. Serve warm.

Baked almond and plum 'cheesecake' (serves 4)

pastry
4oz/100g self raising flour

1½oz/40g vegan margarine

soya milk

filling
3 plums, stoned and thinly sliced

1 dessertspoon brown sugar

4oz/100g vegan 'cream cheese'

1oz/25g raisins, chopped

1oz/25g ground almonds

1oz/25g self raising flour

1 teaspoon almond essence

3 tablespoons soya milk

flaked almonds

Make the pastry by rubbing the margarine into the flour and adding enough soya milk to bind. Turn out onto a floured board and roll out to line a greased loose-bottomed 7 inch/18cm round flan tin. Prick the base with a fork and bake blind in a preheated oven at 180°C/350°F/Gas mark 4 for 5 minutes. Mix the 'cream cheese', raisins, ground almonds, flour, almond essence and soya milk until well combined. Arrange the plum slices in a circular pattern over the base of the flan case, sprinkle with the sugar, then spoon the 'cream cheese' mixture evenly on top, making sure that it touches the pastry all round. Sprinkle the top with flaked almonds and return to the oven for 20-25 minutes until golden. Serve warm, topped with yoghurt or a sweet sauce.

Bulgarian 'milk' pudding (serves 4)

2oz/50g semolina

1oz/25g sultanas

1oz/25g brown sugar

1 dessertspoon vegan margarine

2 fl.oz/50ml fresh apple juice

16 fl.oz/475ml soya milk

1 tablespoon rose water

fresh rose petals

Soak the sultanas in the apple juice for 30 minutes. Melt the margarine, then remove from the heat and add the semolina, sugar, sultanas and remaining juice and mix well. Gradually add the soya milk, stirring between additions until smooth. Bring to the boil while stirring and continue stirring while simmering for 3 minutes, then mix in the rose water and simmer for a further minute. Divide between 4 glass dishes and serve warm or chilled, garnished with fresh rose petals.

Czech plum dumplings (serves 6)

12 plums

brown sugar

ground cinnamon

pastry

8oz/225g plain flour

5oz/150g potato, scraped

1½oz/40g vegan margarine

soya milk

crumb mix

2oz/50g breadcrumbs

1 rounded teaspoon vegan margarine

½ teaspoon ground cinnamon

Boil the potato, drain and dry off over a low heat and mash. Rub the margarine into the flour, add the mashed potato and mix thoroughly. Add a little soya milk to bind, then turn out onto a floured board and knead well. Roll the dough out to an oblong of 9 x 12 inches/23x30cm and cut this into twelve 3 inch/8cm squares.

Cut the plums in half and remove the stones. Sprinkle sugar and ground cinnamon on one half of each plum and replace the other half. Put a whole plum on each of the pastry squares and shape the pastry around it to enclose completely. Bring a large pan of water to the boil, add the dumplings and simmer for 10 minutes.

Meanwhile melt the margarine for the crumb mix in a small pan and stir in the breadcrumbs and ground cinnamon. Transfer the crumb mixture to a plate. Take out the cooked dumplings with a slotted spoon and roll them in the crumbs until covered. Serve hot, topped with 'sour cream' or a sweet sauce.

Stuffed baked apples (serves 4)

4 firm green-skinned eating apples, cored

1oz/25g walnuts, finely chopped

1oz/25g sultanas, finely chopped

1 rounded tablespoon golden syrup

½ teaspoon ground cinnamon

1 dessertspoon lemon juice

Prick the apples a few times with a fork to prevent the skins splitting and put them in a baking dish. Heat the golden syrup gently until runny in a small pan. Remove from the heat and add the walnuts, sultanas, cinnamon and lemon juice. Mix thoroughly, then divide between the centres of the apples, pressing the filling down firmly as you go. Bake in a preheated oven at 180°C/350°F/Gas mark 4 for about 20 minutes until the apples are soft. Serve hot, topped with yoghurt or 'sour cream'.

Autumn fruit cup with chestnut ice (serves 4)

fruit cup

12oz/350g plums, stoned and chopped

8oz/225g eating apple, peeled, cored and diced

8oz/225g dessert pears, peeled, cored and diced

1oz/25g brown sugar

6 cloves

1 tablespoon water

ground cinnamon

chestnut ice

9 fl.oz/250ml soya 'cream'

6oz/175g sweetened chestnut purée

1 teaspoon vanilla essence

Blend the ingredients for the chestnut ice until smooth and pour into a freezerproof container. Cover and freeze for 1 hour. Whisk the mixture, then put it back in the freezer for a few hours until just frozen.

Cook the plums, apples, pears, sugar, cloves and water gently until the fruit is just soft. Transfer to a lidded container and refrigerate until cold. Remove the cloves and divide the fruit between 4 glass dishes. Serve topped with the chestnut ice and sprinkled with ground cinnamon. Keep the ice at room temperature for 30 minutes before serving if it has become too solid.

Polish rice cake (serves 6)

4oz/100g long grain rice

5 fl.oz/150ml water

8 fl.oz/225ml soya milk

1 teaspoon vanilla essence

2oz/50g vegan 'cream cheese'

2oz/50g self raising flour

1oz/25g vegan margarine

½oz/15g brown sugar

½oz/15g walnuts, finely chopped

Put the rice and water in a pan and bring to the boil. Simmer until the liquid has been absorbed, then add the soya milk and vanilla. Bring back to the boil and simmer gently until the soya milk has been absorbed. Add the 'cream cheese', margarine and sugar and stir until melted and well combined. Remove from the heat and mix in the flour, then spoon the mixture into a lined and greased 7 inch/18cm diameter flan tin. Press down evenly and sprinkle the walnuts over the top, pressing them in lightly with the back of a spoon. Bake in a preheated oven at 180°C/350°F/Gas mark 4 for about 30 minutes until golden brown. Carefully turn out of the tin and remove the lining. Cut into wedges and serve warm, topped with yoghurt or stewed fruit.

Apple and cinnamon pancakes (serves 4)

8oz/225g eating apples, peeled, cored and finely chopped

5 fl.oz/150ml soya milk

2½oz/65g plain flour

½ teaspoon ground cinnamon

vegan margarine

lemon juice

brown sugar

extra ground cinnamon

Whisk the flour and ½ teaspoonful of cinnamon with the soya milk until smooth, then stir in the apple. Heat a small amount of margarine in a non-stick frying pan until hot. Drop rounded tablespoonfuls of the apple batter into the pan and cook for a few minutes on each side until golden. Serve hot, sprinkled with lemon juice, brown sugar and ground cinnamon, or top with yoghurt, stewed fruit or a sweet sauce.

Apricot and hazelnut streusel (serves 6)

base

4oz/100g self raising flour

1½oz/40g vegan margarine

soya milk

filling

4oz/100g dried apricots, finely chopped

5 fl.oz/150ml fresh apple juice

topping

2oz/50g self raising flour

1oz/25g hazelnuts, finely chopped

1oz/25g vegan margarine

1oz/25g brown sugar

Soak the apricots in the apple juice for 30 minutes, then cook gently until the liquid has been absorbed. Remove from the heat and mash the apricots.

Rub the margarine into the flour for the base, then add enough soya milk to make a soft dough. Turn out onto a floured board and roll out to fit the base of a base-lined and greased 7 inch/18cm square baking tin. Prick the dough with a fork and bake blind in a preheated oven at 180°C/350°F/Gas mark 4 for 5 minutes.

Melt the margarine for the topping in a small pan, then remove from the heat and stir in the flour, hazelnuts and sugar. Combine well until the mixture is crumbly. Spoon the apricots evenly over the base and spread the topping on top. Press down lightly and return to the oven for 20-25 minutes until browned. Cut into slices and serve hot, topped with yoghurt or a sweet sauce.

BAKING

Home-baked cakes and biscuits are very popular all over the region and variations of some recipes appear in every country. As well as being enjoyed with tea and coffee at home, cakes and biscuits are also served in the numerous coffee houses and milk bars found in towns and cities, while freshly-made jam doughnuts are a favourite snack to buy from street vendors. Almonds, hazelnuts, walnuts, dried apricots and prunes are essential ingredients in many recipes and ground poppy seeds make an unusual filling for a traditional pastry roll which reputedly originated in Hungary but is now a favourite in other countries too. All of the following can be successfully frozen.

Hungarian apple cake

8oz/225g plain flour

2oz/50g vegan margarine, melted

2oz/50g brown sugar

2 eating apples

1 teaspoon easy-blend yeast

approx. 3 fl.oz/75ml soya milk, warmed

1 teaspoon brown sugar

¼ teaspoon ground cinnamon

Mix the flour with the yeast and 2oz/50g of sugar. Peel, core and finely chop one of the apples and add to the bowl together with the margarine. Combine well, then add enough soya milk to make a soft dough. Turn out onto a floured board, knead well and return to the bowl. Cover and allow to rise for an hour in a warm place. Knead the dough again and put it in a greased round 7 inch/18cm baking tin, pressing it out to fill the tin. Cover and leave in a warm place for 40 minutes. Peel, core and slice the other apple and arrange the slices in a circular pattern on top of the cake, pressing them lightly into the dough. Mix the teaspoonful of sugar with the cinnamon and sprinkle over the top. Cover with foil and bake in a preheated oven at 200°C/400°F/Gas mark 6 for 20 minutes. Remove the foil and bake for 10 minutes more, then carefully turn out onto a wire rack to cool before cutting into slices or wedges.

Spiced walnut biscuits (makes approx. 18)

4oz/100g walnuts, grated

4oz/100g breadcrumbs

2oz/50g plain flour

2oz/50g vegan margarine

2oz/50g soft brown sugar

½ teaspoon ground cloves

½ teaspoon ground cinnamon

4 tablespoons soya milk

Cream the margarine with the sugar and work in the walnuts, breadcrumbs and sifted flour and spices until crumbly. Add the soya milk and mix until everything binds together. Take rounded dessertspoonfuls of the mixture and roll into balls, flatten these and put them on a greased baking sheet. Indent the top of each biscuit with a fork and neaten the edges. Bake in a preheated oven at 180°C/350°F/Gas mark 4 for 12-15 minutes until golden brown. Slide onto a wire rack and allow to cool.

Savoury potato pastry twists (makes approx. 10)

4oz/100g potato, peeled
4oz/100g plain flour
1½oz/40g vegan margarine
½oz/15g vegan 'cheese', grated
½ teaspoon paprika
¼ teaspoon caraway seeds
black pepper
1 dessertspoon water

Boil the potato, drain and dry off over a low heat and mash it. Rub the margarine into the flour, then stir in the 'cheese', paprika and caraway seeds, work in the potato and season with black pepper. Now add the water and mix until a soft dough forms. Turn out onto a floured board and roll out to about ⅜ inch/8mm thick. Cut into strips of 5 x ¾ inches/13x2cm. Carefully lift the pastry strips and twist them a couple of times before putting them on a greased baking sheet. Bake in a preheated oven at 180°C/350°F/Gas mark 4 for 15-18 minutes until golden. Transfer to a wire rack to cool.

Slovakian prune and walnut roll (makes 6)

dough

6oz/175g plain flour

1oz/25g vegan margarine

pinch of salt

1 teaspoon easy-blend yeast

approx. 2½ fl.oz/62ml soya milk, warmed

extra soya milk

filling

4oz/100g pitted prunes, finely chopped

4 fl.oz/125ml water

1oz/25g walnuts, finely chopped

Put the prunes and water in a small pan and bring to the boil, cover and simmer until the liquid has been absorbed and the mixture is thick. Remove from the heat and allow to cool.

Mix the flour, salt and yeast in a large bowl, rub in the margarine and gradually add the warmed soya milk until everything binds together. Knead the dough well, then return it to the bowl, cover and leave in a warm place for 30 minutes. Turn the dough out onto a floured board and roll out into a 9 inch/23cm square. Spread the prunes over the dough, leaving a 1 inch/2.5cm gap along one of the edges for joining. Sprinkle the walnuts evenly over the prunes. Starting at the edge opposite the one which has been left free of filling, roll up the dough like a Swiss roll to enclose the filling. Put the roll with the seam underneath on a greased baking sheet and leave in a warm place for 30 minutes. Brush the roll with soya milk and bake in a preheated oven at 180°C/350°F/Gas mark 4 for about 25 minutes until golden brown. Transfer to a wire rack and allow to cool before cutting into thick slices.

Almond and vanilla crescents (makes approx. 24)

2oz/50g ground almonds

2oz/50g plain flour

2oz/50g vegan margarine

1oz/25g brown sugar, lightly ground

1 teaspoon vanilla essence

Cream the margarine with the sugar and vanilla in a mixing bowl, then work in the ground almonds and flour until a soft dough forms. Knead the dough well and turn out onto a floured board. Roll out to approximately ¼ inch/5mm thick and cut into small crescent shapes with a biscuit cutter. Gather up and re-roll the dough until it is all used. Place the crescents on a greased baking sheet and bake in a preheated oven at 180°C/350°F/Gas mark 4 for 8-10 minutes until browned. Allow to cool for 10 minutes, then carefully slide onto a wire rack to cool completely.

Jam doughnuts (makes 8)

8oz/225g plain flour

1 rounded teaspoon easy-blend yeast

½ teaspoon salt

1 tablespoon brown sugar

8 teaspoons sugar-free jam

approx. 4½ fl.oz/137ml soya milk, warmed

vegetable oil

ground cinnamon

Mix the flour with the yeast, salt and sugar in a large bowl. Gradually add the soya milk, to form a soft dough. Turn out onto a floured board and knead for 5 minutes. Return to the bowl, cover and leave in a warm place for 1 hour. Knead the dough again, then divide it into 8 equal portions. Form each portion into a little cup and put a teaspoonful of jam in the centre. Dampen the edges of the dough with water and join them together to enclose the filling. Reshape into balls and place on a greased baking sheet. Leave in a warm place for 40 minutes to rise, then deep fry in hot oil for about 5 minutes until golden. Drain the doughnuts well on kitchen paper and serve warm, sprinkled with ground cinnamon.

Hazelnut cake

4oz/100g breadcrumbs

4oz/100g plain wholemeal flour

2oz/50g hazelnuts, toasted and ground

2oz/50g vegan margarine

1oz/25g brown sugar

1 rounded tablespoon golden syrup

1 rounded teaspoon baking powder

5 fl.oz/150ml soya milk

½oz/15g hazelnuts, chopped

Gently heat the margarine, sugar and golden syrup until melted. Remove from the heat and stir in the breadcrumbs and ground hazelnuts. Add the sifted flour, baking powder and soya milk and mix thoroughly. Spoon the mixture into a lined and greased 7 inch/18cm round baking tin and level the top. Sprinkle the chopped hazelnuts on top and press these in lightly with the back of a spoon. Cover with foil and bake in a preheated oven at 180°C/350°F/Gas mark 4 for 20 minutes. Uncover and bake for another 15 minutes until golden brown. Carefully turn out onto a wire rack and allow to cool.

Apricot and almond squares (makes 9)

6oz/175g self raising flour

2oz/50g ground almonds

2oz/50g vegan margarine

1oz/25g brown sugar

1 teaspoon almond essence

3 tablespoons plain soya yoghurt

soya milk

½oz/15g flaked almonds, finely chopped

filling

4oz/100g dried apricots, finely chopped

6 fl.oz/175ml water

Put the apricots and water in a small pan and bring to the boil. Cover and simmer, stirring occasionally, until the liquid has been absorbed and the apricots are soft. Mash them and set aside to cool.

Cream the margarine with the sugar and almond essence, stir in the ground almonds and flour, then add the yoghurt and mix until a soft dough forms. Take half of the dough and roll it out on a floured board to fit the base of a lined 7 inch/18cm square flan tin. Spread the apricot purée evenly on top and roll out the remaining dough on a floured board to fit over it. Brush the top with soya milk and sprinkle with the chopped flaked almonds, pressing them in lightly with the back of a spoon. Bake in a preheated oven at 180°C/350°F/Gas mark 4 for about 25 minutes until browned, then put on a wire rack to cool before cutting into 9 equal squares.

Spiced cookies (makes approx. 12)

4oz/100g plain flour

1oz/25g vegan margarine

1oz/25g brown sugar

1 rounded tablespoon golden syrup

1 teaspoon ground mixed spice

½ teaspoon baking powder

1 tablespoon soya milk

Heat the golden syrup with the margarine and sugar until melted. Remove from the heat and add the sifted flour, baking powder and mixed spice, stir in the soya milk and mix until everything binds together. Take heaped teaspoonfuls of the mixture and roll into balls. Flatten each ball into a thick round and put these on a greased baking sheet. Indent the tops with a fork and bake in a preheated oven at 180°C/350°F/Gas mark 4 for about 10 minutes until golden brown. Carefully transfer to a wire rack and allow to cool.

Poppy seed and almond roll (makes 6)

pastry

4oz/100g plain flour

pinch of salt

1 teaspoon easy-blend yeast

½oz/15g vegan margarine, melted

approx. 2 fl.oz/50ml soya milk, warmed

extra soya milk

poppy seeds

filling

2oz/50g poppy seeds, ground

2oz/50g ground almonds

2oz/50g raisins, finely chopped

1oz/25g vegan margarine

1 rounded tablespoon golden syrup

1 rounded tablespoon sugar-free apricot jam

1 tablespoon lemon juice

1 tablespoon soya milk

Mix the flour, salt and yeast in a large bowl. Stir in the melted margarine, then gradually add the soya milk until a soft dough forms. Knead the dough well, return it to the bowl, cover and leave in a warm place for 1 hour to rise.

Meanwhile melt the margarine for the filling with the golden syrup. Remove from the heat, add the rest of the filling ingredients and combine well.

Knead the dough again, then roll it out on a floured board into an oblong of 9 x 6 inches/23 x 15cm. Spread the filling evenly over the dough and fold the two long edges towards the centre. Dampen them with soya milk and press together to join. Transfer the roll to a greased baking sheet and leave in a warm place for 20 minutes, then brush with soya milk and sprinkle with poppy seeds. Bake in a preheated oven at 180°C/350°F/Gas mark 4 for about 20 minutes until golden. Allow to cool on a wire rack and serve cut into thick slices.

Chocolate, chestnut and walnut torte

9oz/250g self raising flour

2oz/50g walnuts, grated

1½oz/40g brown sugar

1 rounded tablespoon golden syrup

1 rounded tablespoon cocoa powder

6 fl.oz/175ml sunflower oil

7 fl.oz/200ml soya milk

filling

12oz/350g tinned sweetened chestnut purée, mashed

topping

4oz/100g vegan chocolate bar, broken

walnut halves

Put the sugar, golden syrup, cocoa powder, sunflower oil and soya milk in a mixing bowl and whisk until well combined. Stir in the grated walnuts and flour and combine thoroughly until smooth. Divide the mixture between 2 lined and greased 7 inch/18cm round cake tins and spread out evenly. Bake in a preheated oven at 180°C/350°F/Gas mark 4 for 20-22 minutes until the sponges feel springy in the centre. Carefully turn out onto a wire rack. When cool cut the sponges in half using a sharp knife, to make four thin sponges. Put one of these on a plate and fork a third of the chestnut purée evenly over the top. Repeat these layers twice, finishing with the remaining sponge. Forking the purée rather than spreading it smoothly helps the layers stick together.

Melt the chocolate in a bowl over a pan of boiling water and spread it evenly over the top and sides of the cake. Press the walnut halves in the top, then refrigerate for a couple of hours until the chocolate sets before cutting the cake into wedges.

Almond and yoghurt cookies
(makes approx. 20)

4oz/100g plain flour

2oz/50g ground almonds

2oz/50g vegan margarine

1½oz/40g brown sugar, lightly ground

2 rounded tablespoons plain soya yoghurt

½ teaspoon baking powder

½ teaspoon almond essence

approx. 20 almonds halves

Cream the margarine with the sugar and almond essence, work in the ground almonds, then add the sifted flour and baking powder and yoghurt. Combine until the mixture binds together, then take heaped teaspoonfuls and roll into balls. Flatten the balls and put them on a greased baking sheet. Press an almond half into the top of each one and bake them in a preheated oven at 180°C/350°F/Gas mark 4 for about 15 minutes until golden brown. Slide onto a wire rack to cool.